CORVETTE

CORVETTE

AN AMERICAN CLASSIC

JOHN F. KATZ

Illustrated
Books

A FRIEDMAN GROUP BOOK

BDD Illustrated Books
An imprint of BDD Promotional Book Company, Inc.
1540 Broadway
New York, N.Y. 10036

BDD Illustrated Books and the accompanying logo are trdemarks of
the BDD Promotional Book Company, Inc.

First Published in the United States of America in 1993 by
BDD Illustrated Books.

ISBN 0-7924-5760-9

CORVETTE
An American Classic
was prepared and produced by
Michael Friedman Publishing Group, Inc.
15 West 26th Street
New York, New York 10010

Editor: Dana Rosen
Art Director: Jeff Batzli
Designer: Kevin Ullrich
Photography Editor: Ede Rothaus

Typeset by Classic Type Inc.
Color separations by United South Sea Graphic Art Co.
Printed and bound in China by
Leefung-Asco Printers Ltd.

DEDICATION

For John Victor.

ACKNOWLEDGMENTS

Thanks first of all to my wife and son, who endured temporary widow- and orphanhood while this book monopolized my time and attention.

That said, I would also like to thank Lowell Paddock for an opportunity I desperately needed; Kim M. Miller of the AACA Library and Research Center for her always generous help; Dave Hederich, Mark Broderick, and Kari St. Antoine of Chevrolet; and Henry Siegle, whose fabulous collection of historic automotive literature made this project possible.

This cutaway view of a 1991 ZR-1 shows the elaborate intake manifold of the LT5 engine, with a separate runner for each of the sixteen intake valves. It also reveals much of the unique architecture of the new-generation Corvette, including its aluminum suspension arms, transverse plastic springs, and the aluminum girder that connects the transmission casing to the differential, making the entire driveline a self-supporting unit.

CONTENTS

THE TAO OF THE CORVETTE

The Corvette is you, whoever you are.
William L. Mitchell
From *Corvette, A Piece of the Action*

At twilight, the concrete canyons of northeast Ohio become surreal. The harsh, green-blue glow of the mercury vapor lamps scatters and dances eerily in the deeply polished paint, rippling and stretching over every contour of the long fiberglass hood. Ripping and booming, the exhaust noise reflects from the wall on my left, ricochets around under bridges and inside my head, and then trails off behind me, as the thundering, fuel-injected juggernaut drags me relentlessly toward the horizon.

STOP AHEAD, PAY TOLL commands a large sheet of steel beside the road. The thunder subsides as I lift my foot from the Go pedal to the Stop pedal. Dull-eyed and bored, the weary toll taker doesn't see the cars or even

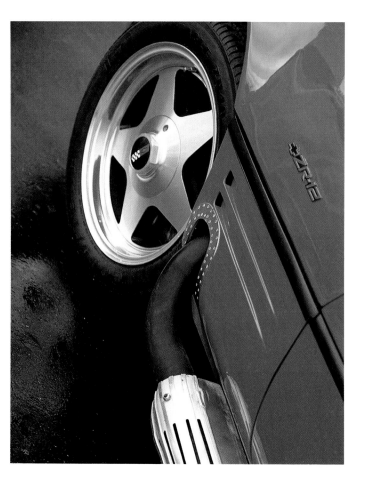

Page 8: The last and, some would say, purest, of the Sting Rays. This 1967 big-block roadster features optional aluminum wheels and side-mounted exhaust. Page 9: The "spinner" wheel cover of the 1956–62 Corvette. For forty years, these crossed flags have stood for America's only true sports car. Right: This is where the thunder comes out: the side-mounted exhaust of the mighty Falconer ZR-12.

the drivers as she transfers wealth from their hands into Ohio's coffers.

But she looks up at the Corvette. And as I hand over my change, she looks straight into my eyes and smiles.

Other cars cling tenaciously to curves and accelerate with wild, bellowing abandon. Other cars have been shaped by passionate artists. Other cars have been winning races for decades, and go on winning today.

But no other car would have elicited that reaction, from that person, in that place and time. It is the Corvette's glory, and its curse.

Like the homegrown racing specials that occasionally embarrassed the rich boys' Ferraris and Maseratis on the airport circuits of the fifties, the Corvette has had to outrun Europe's most exotic automotive machinery using only ingenuity and mass-produced components. It's a tough assignment, and it has required some compromises along the way.

General Motors wouldn't build the Corvette at all if it couldn't build enough of them to make a profit. And not everyone who wants a Corvette necessarily wants a race car. Historically, most buyers have opted for the *least* potent engine available in any given year, or the engine that was one notch up on the option sheet. Only 1,040 people ordered fuel-injected Corvettes in 1957, the year Chevrolet introduced that famous feature. Only 199 bought race-ready Z06 coupes in 1963. Since then, Chevrolet has sold 216 L88s, 28 original ZR1s, 2 ZL1s, and 12 ZR2s. Out of the more than one million Corvettes assembled since 1953, that isn't very many legendary ground-pounders.

So when *Road & Track* complained in December 1964 that the gliterati bought Corvettes for "nymphet nabbing," they might have been right. But are all the Ferrari and Porsches out there really purchased purely out of appreciation for their mechanical excellence? It is worth

remembering that no Corvette, no matter how laden with luxury doodads or smog gear or both, has ever been slow And that the mildest 'Vettes were frequently the best balanced, most practical, and most desirable of fast touring cars.

That's the essential paradox of the Corvette: it has to be safe enough on the street for the unskilled driver, yet fast enough on the track to defeat cars that cost twice as much. It has to ride the cutting edges of both style and engineering—while appealing to a broad enough audience to pay for the tooling. No other car has ever been asked to play as many conflicting roles.

Perhaps this explains the somewhat schizophrenic response that the motoring press has reserved for this car alone. Few other automobiles have been so highly praised, or so resolutely damned—at least not in adjacent paragraphs. For forty years, my colleagues have loved this fiberglass mistress for what she is, hated her for what she is not, and berated her for not becoming what she never could be.

As much as possible, I've tried to tell this tale from their point of view, to locate the Corvette in its historic context. The story has been as wild a ride as the car itself—and I hope you enjoy it as much as I have.

Nicknamed "Conan" by Chevrolet engineers, the experimental ZR-12 was powered by what was essentially one and a half LT5 engines. Veteran Chevrolet race tuner Ryan Falconer built the all-aluminum V12, and the nose of this Corvette coupe was stretched by eight inches to make it all fit.

CHAPTER ONE

THE COUNTRY CLUB CORVETTE, 1953-55

*Considering the statistics, the American
public does not want a sports car
at all....*
Zora Arkus-Duntov, 1953

O f course, Duntov didn't believe that the statistics told the whole story. Neither did Harley Earl.

Imposing at six feet, four inches, Earl spoke with a slow drawl that belied his quick wit. Colleagues remember him as irascible, mischievous—and by some accounts occasionally mean. He couldn't draw a straight line with a ruler, but that hadn't stopped him from running one of southern California's most successful custom body shops in the twenties, before General Motors recruited him to head up its new Art & Colour section. Art & Colour was the first automotive styling department in the modern sense, and Earl became the industry's first design vice president in 1940.

One account of the Corvette's origin has Earl chatting with his son and his son's college buddies, some of whom had spurned the traditional large domestic sedan in favor of a sporty import from England. Most of these prodigals claimed they'd buy a U.S. sports car if only a U.S. company would build one.

Whether or not that's so, as early as 1951 Earl was promoting his personal vision of a simple sports car, priced no higher than a Chevrolet sedan and enjoyed by thousands of college students and club racers all over the United States. He had just completed the legendary LeSabre, the elaborately styled, alcohol-injected, two-seat show car that would define U.S. auto design for the next decade. Now, with stylists Vincent Kaptur, Sr. and Bill Bloch, draftsman Carl Peebles, and clay modeler Tony Balthasar, Earl started work on his $1,850 sports car.

Shortly afterward, Earl came upon a little one-off sportster with a fiberglass body and the unlikely moniker of Alembic I.

Alembic I had been constructed in the spring of 1951 by Glasspar, a California-coast boat builder, at a time when fiberglass wasn't exactly de rigueur for boats, either. Subsequently, the Naugatuck Chemical Division of U.S. Rubber, one of Glasspar's suppliers, acquired the Jeep-based roadster, named it after a benzene compound, and presented it to General Motors in March 1952.

Intrigued, Earl redoubled his own sports-car efforts. A young stylist named Robert F. McLean proposed a 102-inch wheelbase (same as the Jaguar XK-120), with the engine placed three inches lower and seven inches back from its position in a Chevy sedan. With these changes, the concept moved closer to a thoroughbred sports car—and away from the inexpensive, rebodied Chevy that Earl had envisioned. McLean told Earl that that was how the British did it, and Earl bought the idea on the spot. The crew completed a full-size clay model based on these proportions by the end of April and then prepared a plaster model to present to management.

At that time, management was yearning for something new for Chevrolet, whose image was growing dowdier by the year. (In July 1953, Tom McCahill would describe the Chevrolet sedan as a "friendly old toothbrush.") Chevy still outsold Ford in 1952, but Dearborn was closing fast, and outgoing GM president Charlie Wilson asked Chevrolet sales manager Thomas H. Keating what he needed to widen the gap. Keating himself had noted that Ford already sold more convertibles and wagons than Chevy—a good sign that younger people were shopping across town. He asked Wilson for engineer Ed Cole, who had led the development of Cadillac's high-compression V8 engine and was then managing T-41 tank production in Cleveland.

Cole enjoyed sports cars; he had owned an XK-120 Jaguar and a Cadillac-powered Allard. He had barely arrived at Chevrolet when he was ushered into the styling auditorium, along with Keating and new GM President Harlow "Red" Curtice. Legend has it that Cole literally jumped up and down at the sight of the plaster sports car. He and Keating wanted it for Chevrolet's stand at the next Motorama—and possibly for production as well.

On June 2, Cole and Keating showed the plaster model to Research and Development chief Maurice Olley, and they assigned him to design a chassis that would fit the existing contours and that would be ready for the Motorama in seven months—and for the assembly line in twelve. And oh, yes, he was instructed to be sure to keep the cost down, too.

An Englishman by birth, Olley had moved to the United States with the Rolls-Royce company's Springfield, Massachusetts, operation, and he had elected to stay when Rolls packed up the shop and returned all manufacturing to England. In the early thirties, he had pioneered the simple but effective asymmetric wishbone suspension layout that—despite Earl MacPherson's struts—remains the standard of the world today.

In a paper presented to the Society of Automotive Engineers in Detroit on October 5, 1953, Olley outlined his goals for the car that became the Corvette:
- a cruising speed over 70 mph
- weight-to-power ratio better than 25 lb/bhp
- quick steering without oversteer
- low center of gravity
- minimum overhang, with low moment of inertia relative to wheelbase

Further, wrote Olley, "A joggling ride is not acceptable, but a floating ride which appears to be divorced from the road is even more unacceptable. Excessive roll and vague handling characteristics will not do."

By June 12, 1952, Olley had completed a rear three-quarter overhead sketch of the definitive Corvette chassis, right down to the reshaped rocker-arm cover that allowed the low hood line. He had labeled the sketch "Opel"—a credible ruse, since Chevrolet engineering sometimes consulted on projects for the German GM operation. Olley used off-the-shelf components wherever possible, incorporating not only the front suspension of the Chevy sedan but also the crossmember that went with it. He even retained the standard front springs (they would be "stiffer" relative to the lighter body), although he did specify a bigger antiroll bar.

But the very proportions of the Corvette demanded certain departures from standard Chevrolet practice. The wheelbase, for example, was too short for a torque tube (the drive shaft would be only thirty-six inches long), so Olley chose an open propeller shaft with "Hotchkiss drive" through the springs. And since the fiberglass body would add virtually nothing to overall rigidity, Olley designed a new box-section frame with a central crossmember lying below the drive shaft.

Other choices seem quaint today. "We are aware of a preference for rack and pinion steering on cars of this type," wrote Olley. "However, this involves a steering ratio of the order of 9 or 10 to 1. We regard this as too fast even for a sports car...." The Corvette used a Saginaw worm-and-sector steering box, with the idler arm redesigned to clear the low-mounted engine. Interestingly, Olley also designed some passive rear-wheel steering into the chassis by tipping the rear end of the rear leaf springs sharply upward.

On paper at least, the design succeeded. Combined with the lighter body, the relocated engine reduced polar moment of inertia (relative to a Chevrolet sedan) by 38 percent. The Corvette's center of gravity rode just eighteen inches above the road.

This was the instrument pod of the future in 1953. The blending of the dashboard, door, and windshield-frame shapes has come back in vogue on today's sporty coupes.

Meanwhile, Cole and an assistant named Harry Barr busied themselves in the engine bay. Chevrolet's four-bearing, overhead-valve six hadn't changed much since the late thirties, and now it would have to power a modern sports car. A compression ratio of 8.0:1 (versus 7.1:1 on manual-shift sedans and 7.5:1 on automatics) combined with a higher-lift camshaft, triple side-draft Carters, and revised manifolding, boosted horsepower from 108 to 150, while fattening up the torque curve from idle all the way to 4400 rpm.

The dual exhaust manifolds alone added 8 to 10 pound-feet of torque. Said the redoubtable Olley: "A requirement in the minds of sports car enthusiasts is that the exhaust should have the right note. They don't agree what this is. Some prefer 'foo-blap' while other go for 'foo-gobble.' It is impossible to please them all. We hope we have achieved a desirable compromise." Even the ignition system was unique to the Corvette, designed to operate over 5000 rpm if necessary.

Of course, the most controversial feature of the early Corvette was its Powerglide transmission—with no manual option. Other writers have tried to account for this, suggesting, quite logically, that the automatic transmission represented "high technology" in 1953, so naturally Chevrolet management perceived it as an appropriate feature for a futuristic sports car. Chevrolet had been the first in the low-priced field to offer an automatic transmission, in 1950, and this was no doubt a point of pride in the division. Further, the company always offered its most powerful engine and automatic transmission together as an exclusive package.

Whatever the real reason for the decision, however, Olley defended it in his usual style: "The typical sports car enthusiast, like the 'average man' or the square root of minus one, is an imaginary quantity. Also, as the sports car appeals to a wider section of the public, the center of gravity of this theoretical individual is shifting from the austerity of the pioneer towards the luxury of modern ideas."

Earl himself picked the name "Corvette." Designer Bill Mitchell wrote years later that no one else particularly liked it at the time. But it was already on the prototype when it debuted at New York's Waldorf-Astoria hotel in January 1953. "It is named after the trim, fleet naval vessel that performed heroic escort and patrol duties in World War II," explained the official publicity. As Mitchell pointed out, the car gave the name its glamor, not the other way around. Management had considered calling the new car "Corvair."

By that time, Chevrolet Engineering already had assembled a few complete Corvettes for testing. The design evolved somewhat from that of the show car. The deck lid now hinged in two pieces, with separate openings for the trunk and the top. The prototype's vaguely nautical cowl vents disappeared, as did its exterior door

buttons. The funny little dart on the front fender of the show car was inverted, moved under the Chevrolet script, and extended so that it stretched between the front and rear wheel openings.

Despite Alembic I, GM originally intended to produce the Corvette with a steel body. But the car's overwhelmingly positive reception at shows around the country convinced management to build 300 units in fiberglass while the steel tooling was on order. Somewhere along the line, they decided to stick with fiberglass. No doubt some energetic lobbying from Naugatuck Chemical influenced that decision. But there was another reason: "People seemed to be captivated by the idea of the fiberglass plastic body," Chevrolet body engineer Ellis "Jim" Premo told Karl Ludvigsen, author of *Corvette: America's Star-Spangled Sports Car.* Captivating people is what sports cars are for.

When GM sought bids on fiberglass body panels, it specified 1,000 per month by calendar year 1954,

clearly expecting to sell a lot of Corvettes. Production finally began in June 1953. On June thirtieth, Chevrolet issued a rather unconvincingly posed press photo showing three Corvettes on an "assembly line." Around the same time, Chevrolet announced a base price of $3,250—nearly twice what Earl had hoped for. It would rise to $3,498 before the year was out.

In fact, the "line" in Flint, Michigan, was only six cars long, and by August it had completed only thirteen examples. Four of those were snapped up by Curtice and other GM execs, and the engineers kept the remaining nine for testing, leading *Motor Trend* to quip that "the hoped-for output of 300 additional units this year will scarcely take care of the top GM brass."

The Flint assembly line never produced more than three cars a day; that was as fast as the Molded Fiber Glass Body Company of Ashtabula, Ohio, could provide the panels. Every one of them was painted "polo white" and fitted with a red interior; Chevrolet wouldn't add a

An early '53 with its weather protection in place. The removable side curtains incorporated wind wings, which allowed access to the inside door handles.

second color ("pennant blue") until large-scale production began in St. Louis in December.

With production starting so late in the year, Keating, now general manager of Chevrolet, promised Corvettes only to "principal dealers" for the remainder of the year. New Chevy sales manager William E. Fish suggested that the few Corvettes available be reserved for "prestige owners"—celebrities, civic leaders, high-profile businesspeople, and the like. Unfortunately, the number of VIPs looking to buy sports cars proved to be even lower than the number of available Corvettes, and despite one bold announcement that 1953 production had sold out by August, Chevrolet had in fact unloaded only 183 of the 300 'Vettes by year's end. But Chevrolet stuck stubbornly by its VIP-only marketing policy until the summer of 1954. Production slowed drastically in St. Louis, but the year still ended with 1,076 unsold Corvettes languishing on dealers' lots. If Ford hadn't shown a mocked-up but clearly mass-producible Thunderbird in February 1954, GM management surely would have killed the Corvette.

Road & Track voiced a hard-line definition of a sports car when the magazine previewed the Corvette in August 1953: "If you can't race it, *it isn't a sports car!*" Chevrolet, it seems, had made a pronouncement that the Corvette "is not intended to be used as a racing car." An unconfirmed rumor said that GM had turned down Briggs Cunningham's order for two of the cars to race at Le Mans. "But Jaguar said the same thing in 1949," noted *R&T*'s scribes, adding that "the Corvette will be used in competition and it has every chance of its share of successes."

The article was accompanied by publicity photos of the Motorama Corvette, indicating that the editors probably hadn't had a chance to drive the real car. Still, they liked what they saw: "Clean functional lines of the Corvette reflect the fact that this is a genuine sports car, a

Chevrolet seems to have gathered roughly 10 percent of the entire year's Corvette output for this 1953 publicity photo.

refreshing contrast to the pseudo sports cars being shown by other divisions of GM.'' They greeted even the Corvette's automatic transmission with a surprisingly open mind: ''The specification of a Powerglide transmission has met with considerable derision but a torque convertor has potential advantages for road racing which have not been fully explored.'' The editors praised the Corvette's fiberglass body for ''excellent workmanship and careful attention to detail.'' They liked the quality of the top, and even the dismal dashboard design seems to have eluded their scorn.

Apparently *Road & Track*'s doubts about the transmission grew after the staff actually drove a Corvette for the June 1954 issue. ''Admittedly it will convert a lot of people to sports cars,'' the editors wrote, ''who have no desire to develop driving skill.'' They fretted, however, about the effect of an unwanted and unexpected downshift while cornering ''at the ragged edge of tire adhesion.''

The two-speed transmission left the 'Vette feeling sluggish off the line, but it still scooted to 60 mph in 11 seconds and passed the quarter-mile mark in 18. Those weren't bad numbers in those days, although the testers commented that the Corvette didn't feel as fast as their stopwatches proved it to be. Although the engine had less than 500 miles on it, they put it through a 12-mile top-speed run; the paint on the block burned, but the Corvette reached a true 106.4 miles per hour.

''The ride is so good that few American car owners would notice much difference from their own cars,'' they commented. ''Yet there is a feeling of firmness about the car, and none of the easy slow motion effect of our large heavy sedans.'' Although it cornered exceptionally flat, the Corvette could be a handful in a drift. Faster steering, the editors suggested, would help. They even defended the Corvette's humble origins, noting that Mercedes-Benz, Porsche, Alfa Romeo, Siata, Lancia, Gordini,

The year 1954 brought only one visible change to the Corvette cockpit: the carpeting and upholstery were now produced in beige (with blue exterior only) and red (with red, white, and black paintwork).

Talbot, and Jaguar had all built successful sports cars from sedan components.

Of course, the Corvette was only part of Keating's master plan for the revival of Chevrolet. More important, he would redesign the entire Chevy line, a project that started in December 1951. That's when Keating convinced GM's Engineering Policy Committee that Chevrolet needed a modern V8 engine—shortly before asking for Ed Cole.

Perhaps a little bored by armored cavalry, Cole had already roughed out a new V8 in Cleveland, establishing its $3\frac{3}{4} \times 3$-inch bore and stroke. He found Chevrolet engineers already hard at work on a smaller V8, but he scrapped that one in May 1952 in favor of his own. By late 1953 Cole had his 265-cubic-inch engine built and running—in the ex-Motorama Corvette! With the prototype thus converted, he convinced GM management to offer the V8 as an option in the '55 Corvette.

Cole's V8 was an innovative design, featuring, among other things, stamped-steel rocker arms to save weight. The hottest version offered in a Chevy sedan, called ''Power Pack,'' sported a four-barrel carburetor and dual exhausts and produced 180 bhp. Cole boosted this to 195 bhp with a high-lift camshaft exclusive to the Corvette. Best of all, the V8 actually weighed forty-one pounds *less* than the old Blue Flame six.

It was a fantastic engine, but by the time it appeared *Road & Track* had simply lost patience with the new Chevrolet sports car. ''The occasional rare appearance of a Corvette in competition has not been marked by any major upset,'' the editors snorted in July 1955. Despite how well they worked on the street, the Corvette's brakes just weren't adequate for piling into a tight road-course corner. And coming out of the turns, 2-liter European cars left the 3.8-liter Chevy behind. Readers had complained about inadequate weather sealing, and the editors finally

noticed just how hard it was to read any gauge save the speedometer while the car was actually moving. Almost grudgingly, they praised the Corvette's "excellent" ride and "near-perfect" directional stability.

"The amazing thing about the Corvette," *R&T* concluded, "is that it comes so close to being a really interesting, worthwhile and genuine sports car—yet misses the mark almost entirely."

Even with the V8, the Corvette still looked like a loser to GM managers, who wanted the whole project stopped before it cost any more money. "But we loved that car," Cole told a reporter at the time. "We weren't going to let it go."

Left: The Corvette engine benefited from a number of running improvements during 1954. Although the decal on the valve cover didn't change, later models produced 155 bhp, thanks to a revised camshaft. And the dual air cleaners shown here, added to the last 735 cars built during the model year, replaced the original three-bullet design, at last solving the engine-fire problem that afflicted earlier 'Vettes. Bottom left: Chevrolet added Black, Pennant Blue, and the Sportsman Red to the Corvette color chart for 1954. The blue, together with Polo White, accounted for 95 percent of all Corvette production that year.

CHAPTER TWO

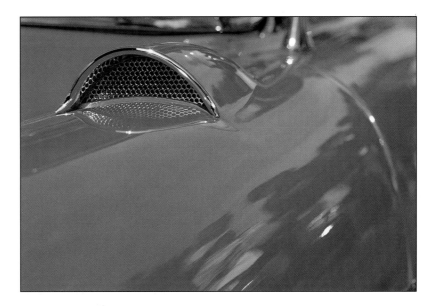

GETTING SERIOUS, 1956-62

Nobody but Chevrolet makes a
luxury car that also is a genuine
100-proof sports car.
Corvette advertisement, 1956

Page 24: Dual headlamps and rakish—but fake—brake cooling scoops characterized the exciting, extroverted, and perhaps a bit overwrought styling of the 1958–60 Corvette. This 1961 model shows a bit more restraint, having at least shed the grille teeth and chromed headlight bezels of previous years. "Wide white" tires were offered for the last time on the '61 'Vette. Page 25: The curious fender-mounted air scoops of the Motorama prototype reappeared on the production Corvette in 1956. The designers had thought them a clever way to direct cool air down into the foot wells. But while GM brass liked the fender blips, they nixed the accompanying ductwork to save production costs.

Born in Belgium of Russian parents, Zora Arkus-Duntov learned to drive as a chauffeur's assistant. He studied engineering in Germany while racing cars and motorcycles in his spare time. As a racing engineer in prewar France, Duntov watched the native Talbots and Delahayes challenge the seemingly invincible Mercedes-Benz and Auto Union teams. He conceived his Ardun high-performance cylinder head, he claimed, while driving his flathead Ford flat-out across the countryside. But its resemblance to the pushrod hemi of the Talbot T.150 could hardly be coincidental.

After World War II, Duntov and his brother Yura briefly marketed the Ardun head as well as performance camshafts for Ford and Mercury V8s in the United States. He crossed the Atlantic again and worked for Sydney Allard, and even co-drove with Allard—unsuccessfully—at Le Mans. The fall of 1952 found Duntov back in the United States, looking for work.

Duntov spotted the prototype Corvette at the New York Motorama and immediately saw its potential. He wrote to Ed Cole about the car, and at least partly because of that letter, Maurice Olley hired him for Chevrolet Engineering in May 1953. By July, Duntov had maneuvered himself into the department responsible for developing the Corvette. Still, he took time off to return to Le Mans, where he co-drove Porsche Spyders to 1100cc class victories in 1954 and 1955.

Later, Duntov was appointed director of High Performance Vehicle Design and Development. Only then did the Corvette become his primary responsibility, although he was still expected to develop special engine and chassis projects for other Chevrolet models. Even today, after living in the United States for half a century, he speaks with a unique accent, his English words filtered through several European languages. It is because of Duntov, mainly, that the Corvette is like no other American car.

Even before Corvette production began, Duntov had been rethinking Olley's suspension design. He had driven an engineering prototype and was dissatisfied with the way it handled when he pushed it hard. By limiting rear spring travel and installing an even larger stabilizer at the front, he was able to reduce oversteer at the limit.

Olley had balanced the Corvette's handling by designing oversteer into the front end and understeer into the rear. But Duntov saw little sense in the two ends fighting each other when they could work better in harmony. He shimmed the front crossmember for more caster angle; further shimming of the central idler arm took out the roll oversteer. In the rear, new hangers flattened out the springs and eliminated roll understeer.

Owners had complained about exhaust fumes in the car, and with a little aerodynamic experimentation Duntov found that opening the wind wings sucked the exhaust forward into the cockpit. Relocating the exhaust tips to the outboard edges of the fenders solved the problem.

But these changes would not see production before 1956. In March 1954, the stylists had worked out a handsome face-lift of the original car, intended for the 1955 model year. It incorporated the relocated exhaust tips and an egg-crate grille similar to that of the all-new '55 full-size Chevrolet. But management wouldn't invest in restyling a car that already appeared doomed.

All of that changed in early 1955, when GM decided not only to continue building the Corvette, but to get seri-

Zora Arkus-Duntov had designed race cars in Germany, smuggled gold in France, and marketed high-performance equipment for Fords in the United States of America. But the first Corvette so impressed this immigrant engineer that he applied for work at Chevrolet, writing to Chief Engineer Ed Cole directly. Within two months Duntov had been hired and was already swatting technical bugs in the nascent sports car. The Corvette SS shown here resulted from one of his earliest attempts to evolve a world-class sports-racer from the Corvette concept. Ultimately, he would guide Corvette development for more than two decades.

A detachable hardtop first appeared on a Corvette Motorama prototype in 1954 and reached production almost unchanged in 1956. Restyled with the rest of the car in 1963 and 1968, the hardtop remained a Corvette extra through 1975—and returned to the option list in 1989.

ous about it as well. Duntov's suspension changes were approved for 1956 production. The brake lining material was changed to reduce both fade and wear. And the standard transmission would be a three-speed manual. (A stick shift had been theoretically available for both the six and the V8 in 1955, but fewer than two dozen units— all of them V8s—were actually built.)

With ratios of 2.2:1 in first and 1.31:1 in second, the 1956 gearbox effectively corresponded to a typical European four-speed with first gear deleted. Having to start in "second" may have slowed the 'Vette a bit off the line, but the three closely spaced ratios were perfect for road racing. *Road & Track* even noted that while the Corvette's first gear was not synchronized, it could be "engaged at 50 or 60 mph without double-clutching."

At the same time, Chevrolet dropped the six-cylinder Corvette entirely. A new compression ratio of 9.25:1

boosted the V8's brake horsepower to 210 at 5200 rpm. Twin four-barrel Carters were optional, raising output to 225 bhp at 5200 rpm and 270 pound-feet of torque at 3000 rpm. *Road & Track* called this an "amazing" number, and noted that, at 0.85 bhp/cubic inch, "the Corvette develops more power for its size than any other American engine."

Of course none of these changes were as visible as the '56 Corvette's breathtaking new styling. Harley Earl's original design was cleaner, perhaps, but it lacked a consistent theme, with its quaint headlamp stone guards at one end and futuristic tailfins at the other. But in 1956 the 'Vette traded in its Motorama image for the more aggressive look of a contemporary, continental sports car. When the 1956 Corvette appeared—unfashionably late in January 1956—the stylists had left not a single panel of the original car unchanged.

At the time, GM's designers were particularly infatuated with the Mercedes-Benz 300 SL. Mitchell, by then Earl's right-hand man, even wanted a gull-wing Corvette, but the engineers objected to the extra weight they thought the upward-opening doors would add. Still the '56 'Vette owed its forward-thrusting front fenders, the two thin longitudinal bulges in its engine hood, and the rakish slope of its de-finned tail to the exotic, Teutonic Mercedes. On the other hand, the concave "coves" in the Corvette's front fenders and doors were inspired by the outwardly flared mudguards found on French sportsters of the twenties. (They had previously appeared on some GM show cars—including the peculiar-looking Biscayne, on which they pointed in the wrong direction.)

The new body at last incorporated exterior door handles and roll-up windows—with power windows as an option, no less. The folding top was power operated and featured more bows than in previous years so that it didn't "fall into your lap," as one pundit put it. Chevrolet even offered a handsome removable hardtop. Only a few details of the new body were disappointing: the Motorama car's periscopic cowl vents had returned—without the ductwork to make them functional. And the old, unreadable dashboard, which R&T now described as "dizzy," remained.

Nit-picking aside, however, the new body made the '56 Corvette "a real traffic stopper," as Ludvigsen wrote in Sports Cars Illustrated, and the most handsome to date—just as Duntov's refinements had made it the best engineered. In March, a factory-backed racing team, fronted by an Illinois speed shop, finished miserably in the 12-hour race at Sebring. Chevrolet advertising, which had previously all but ignored the Corvette, now crowed loudly about the Sebring adventure, ably exploiting the fact that the Corvettes finished at all. For the first time Corvette sales literature became widely available to dealers, and Chevrolet advertised the Corvette on national television.

Then a previously amateur racer, Dr. Richard Thompson, with covert factory support, entered his Corvette at Pebble Beach in April, where he led the Mercedes-Benz 300 SLs and Jaguar XK-140MCs until brake fade forced him to back off in the corners. He still finished second, and he went on to win a point-total championship in the Sports Car Club of America's (SCCA's) C-production class.

"The Corvette as it stands is fully as much a dual-purpose machine as the stock Jaguar, Triumph, or Austin-Healey," Ludvigsen continued. "Without qualification, General Motors is now building a sports car." Still, he complained about mushy seats, a steering wheel that was much too close, and "very little interior room for such a large car." And on the test track, he noted that the Corvette now *understeered* too strongly, and that its new brake linings still allowed an alarming amount of fade.

Even *Road & Track* noted "the tremendous improvement in performance that three years of development has accomplished," rating the new Corvette's "handling qualities and cornering ability…good to excellent." With twin carbs, stick shift, and a 3.55 axle, their test car rocketed to 60 mph in just 7.3 seconds and averaged 129.1 mph in a two-way, maximum-speed run. Corvette production rallied from a mere 700 units in 1955 to a more promising 3467 in 1956.

The year 1957 brought virtually no change in the Corvette's appearance but added an exciting new option under the hood: fuel injection. The idea was not new: during World War II aircraft had used high-pressure fuel delivery to maintain a usable mixture at high altitudes. At one time, fuel injection had been a proposed feature of the star-crossed '48 Tucker, and it had been an ongoing project at GM since the early fifties, under the able supervision of engineer John

Top: The lovely inset taillights of the 1956–57 Corvette replaced the awkward fins of previous years. Up front, the headlights now thrust forward assertively, rather than retreating behind wire-mesh screens. Sports Cars Illustrated called the '56 Corvette "a real traffic stopper." Bottom: The 1957 model, shown here, was virtually identical in appearance. Opposite page: A real fifties fantasy, this 1957 Corvette dash frames competition-style gauges in pastel hues, chrome brightwork, and a bit of forced symmetry.

Dolza. But it first appeared in regular production on the 1954 Mercedes-Benz 300 SL—and GM certainly was watching it closely. The General accelerated its own fuel-injection program after the Mercedes' debut.

Cole, by then a GM vice president as well as Chevrolet general manager, wanted fuel injection not only for the Corvette but for the 1957 full-size Chevies as well. Plymouth and Ford were bringing all-new bodies to market that year, while Chevrolet had only face-lifted '55-'56 models to sell. Cole believed that the high-performance image of fuel injection would compensate for an aging shape on the showroom floor. He reassigned Duntov to assist Dolza, and together they arrived at a constant-injection system with individual nozzles upstream of each intake port. Whereas aircraft systems had metered fuel according to engine speed and air density, the Dolza/Duntov injection system simplified matters by measuring the volume of air entering the engine (as a carburetor does), using a venturi flow meter upstream of the throttle plate.

One prototype system used a stock intake manifold with the metering venturi screwed down where the carburetor should have been. Dynamometer tests indicated that this setup produced exactly the same power and torque curves as a carburetor with equivalent airflow. But subsequent field testing in a '56 Chevy sedan showed dramatically improved acceleration with injection. From this Duntov and Dolza concluded that the injection system allowed the engine to work closer to its theoretical potential throughout its rev range.

Of course, they also knew that fuel injection potentially could deliver higher horsepower because it allowed more exotic manifolds. With fuel delivered directly to the ports, they could optimize the intake tract for airflow and resonance without worrying about fuel distribution or cold-weather condensation. Naturally, the Chevrolet system fully exploited these possibilities, using eight long, nearly vertical intake runners tied together at the top by a shallow plenum chamber. Clever design allowed Chevrolet to use the same low-pressure, diaphragm-type fuel pump on both injected and carbureted cars; a second gear-type pump on injected cars boosted fuel pressure to the necessary level. It nestled next to the fuel distributor and was driven off the ignition distributor by a flexible cable.

Then disaster struck in April 1956: Duntov fractured his spine in a Proving Ground accident. Without him, fuel-injection development ground to a halt.

Fortunately, Duntov suffered no permanent disability and was back at work by the end of June, wearing a brace and wrapped in a skirt (as he could not bend sufficiently to put on pants). Production of the 1957 models had already started by the time the fuel injection system was ready—but the wait proved well worthwhile.

For 1957, the engineers had increased the cylinder bore of the Chevrolet V8 to 3⁷/₈ inches, which brought the displacement to 283 cubic inches. Corvette buyers were offered not one but two versions of this engine with fuel injection. The first, with hydraulic lifters and 9.5:1 compression, produced 250 bhp at 5000 rpm and 305 pound-feet of torque at 3800 rpm. A solid-lifter version with a more radical "Duntov" camshaft (he had developed it for a record attempt at Daytona Beach in 1956) and 10.5:1 compression produced 290 pound-feet of torque at 4400 rpm and 290 bhp at 6200 rpm. Chevrolet advertising gleefully subtracted 7 gross horsepower and bragged that the "283 horsepower" engine produced "one horsepower for every cubic inch."

Two more options that appeared late in the 1957 season helped to build the Corvette legend. The first, in May, was the long-overdue four-speed transmission—in fact a modification of an existing Borg-Warner three-speed, with its reverse gearset relocated to its tail shaft and a

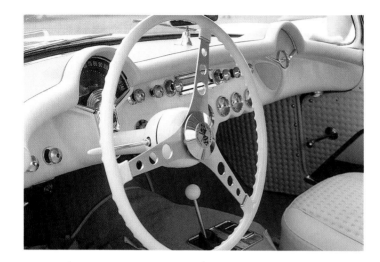

fourth forward ratio installed where reverse had been. The selection of ratios was interesting and reflected Chevrolet's commitment to road racing. First was still a tallish 2.2:1, the same as in the three-speed; second was 1.66:1, and third was 1.31:1, which was the same as second gear in the three-speed.

At the same time Chevrolet offered a heavy-duty suspension and brake package—RPO 684 on the order form —which comprised springs 13 percent stiffer up front and 9 percent stiffer in the rear, bigger shocks at both ends, a 9 percent fatter front antiroll bar, faster-ratio steering (from 3.7 turns lock-to-lock to 2.9), and a limited-slip differential. The brakes supplied with RPO 684 featured finned drums and ventilated backing plates with built-in air scoops, and Bendix Cerametalix brake linings made, as their name suggests, of a ceramic-metal compound.

Dr. Thompson and Gaston Andrey drove a four-speed, fuel-injected RPO 684-equipped Corvette to twelfth place at Sebring—20 laps ahead of the best-placed 300 SL. Other Corvettes finished fifteenth and sixteenth. Thompson went on to win another SCCA national championship, this time in B Production.

It is sobering to remember, however, that of the 6339 Corvettes built in model-year 1957, only 1,040 were equipped with fuel injection—which is not surprising, considering the $481 it added to the 'Vette's base price of $3176. The four-speed transmission cost a more modest $188 but was not available until May of 1957, and RPO 684 cost a whopping $725. Purchased together, these options raised the base price of a new Corvette more than 43 percent—and the number of examples built with all three must have been minuscule.

In fact, not even *Road & Track* could get a Corvette equipped with all three options, finally settling in August 1957 for a road test of a 290-bhp fuel-injected car that had had its four-speed transmission and the rear half of

RPO 684 (rear springs and shocks plus the limited-slip differential) installed by its enthusiastic owner. Not surprisingly, the intrepid testers complained that the distance between second and third gears was too short, but they had nothing but praise for the fuel-injected engine, calling it "an absolute jewel, quiet and remarkably docile when driven gently around town, yet instantly transformable into a roaring brute.... Its best feature is its instantaneous throttle response, completely free of any stumble or stutter under any situation...."

The handsome and successful Corvette of 1956-57 might have continued unmolested for a few more years.

The stylists had worked out a mild face-lift that would have added the prerequisite quad headlamps, plus bogus brake scoops on either side of the grille, to the '56-57 model. But someone at GM's top-level management decided that that wasn't enough.

Caressed by a wide-eyed brunette, a restyled '58 Corvette graced the cover of the December 1957 *Road & Track*. Inside, however, the editors commented acidly about "the corrosive influence of the 'stylists'." The same basic body shape from 1956-57 remained, with the dual-headlight front end, but it had been positively festooned with phony air intakes and exits, all suitably surrounded by heavy-handed chrome moldings. "In the swim with dual headlights," read one caption, "the new model has grown too fussy." But that same criticism could be applied to most U.S. cars in 1958.

At least the new dashboard—redesigned at Duntov's insistence—placed all of the instruments in front of the driver. And the central "control tower" that housed the radio, heater knobs, and clock predicted the center consoles that remain popular today.

The options list reflected Chevrolet's growing realization that some Corvette buyers were more serious about performance than others. A heavy-duty suspension

The Corvette followed an industry-wide trend toward fussier, flashier styling for 1958. Road & Track was appalled, but today many enthusiasts love the Corvettes of this era for their extroverted, aggressive look. Technical improvements included acrylic-lacquer paints and bumpers that attached to the frame rather than the body.

Golden Days

Zora Arkus-Duntov had a good reason for wanting to make his flathead Ford faster. When his family fled Nazi Germany, Duntov left behind a comfortable job as a consultant to Daimler-Benz. He was looking for a way to make a living in France when a friend suggested a lucrative—if illegal—sideline: smuggling gold into Belgium. Recently, Duntov told *Car and Driver* contributing editor Pete Lyons that he stuffed gold coins into a reinforcing tube on his Ford's rear axle. With his driving skill, Duntov could cover the distance from Paris to Brussels in two hours and twenty minutes—which must have been something of a record.

It also allowed him to make the round trip at night, before his parents realized he had left the house....

Opposite page: For 1959, the Corvette shed the '58 model's washboard-style hood louvers and chrome deck-lid ribs for a somewhat cleaner appearance. Above: The '59 Corvette featured a new trailing-arm rear suspension (still with leaf springs, however) and optional sintered-metallic brakes. Other refinements included less reflective instrument lenses, better seats, and even more interior elbowroom thanks to redesigned inner door panels.

package offered front springs 13 percent stiffer than standard—340 versus 300 pounds per inch—and rear spring leaves shored up by 9 percent, from 115 to 125 pounds per inch. Shocks and sway bars were fortified similarly, and the overall steering ratio reduced from 21.0:1 to 16.3:1.

Apparently unfazed by the Corvette's dazzling frills and baubles, *Motor Trend* called it "just the rig for the sports car enthusiast who likes to buy American." Chevrolet sold 9168 of them—and actually made money on the Corvette for the first time.

In 1959, most of the automobile industry retreated, however tentatively they made the effort, from the styling excesses that had characterized the previous year. For the Corvette this meant removing the fake louver panel from the engine hood (several contemporary writers called it "the washboard") and stripping the chrome bars from the trunk lid. Both changes did succeed in help-

ing to relieve the overwrought appearance the Corvette had acquired—if only by a little.

Interior refinements included concave lenses for the instruments, which reduced annoying reflections. The seats were reshaped as well. Duntov told *Sports Car Illustrated*'s Stephen F. Wilder, "In a racing car, the seat is 100 percent for working, just like a stool by a lathe. But in a passenger car, you're lucky if it's a 'work chair' more than 10 percent of the time. It must be easy to get in and out of, and comfortable for lounging in. The high sides of a real bucket seat are just right for holding you in place but they don't meet these other requirements." *Road & Track* thought the chairs in the '59 'Vette were "among the most comfortable seats in any car, sports or otherwise." Duntov also revealed that he had relocated the door handles after driving a '58 'Vette in a borrowed raincoat: the cinch straps on his sleeves had opened the door every time he turned left.

The 1960 Corvette looked virtually identical to the '59; only the upholstery was different. Underneath, however, Duntov added a rear antiroll bar and retuned the standard suspension for greatly improved handling.

Duntov directed more important changes under the skin. Twin trailing links now located the rear axle, which in turn allowed softer, more vertical shock absorbers for a smoother ride with no loss in handling. Moraine sintered-metallic brakes joined the Cerametalix as a heavy-duty brake option. But with front spring rates increased to 550 pounds per inch, the heavy-duty suspension was now suitable for racing only. Even Duntov admitted that "for flat, smooth courses, such as Le Mans or Sebring, the heavy duty suspension option is very effective. But because it is so much stiffer, especially in roll, it would actually be a hindrance on a bumpy circuit such as the Nürburgring." Customers could order the 283 V8 in five different states of tune, from 230 to 290 bhp, depending on compression ratio, carburetion, and cam.

Testing a 290-bhp fuel-injected car with the standard suspension and sintered iron brakes, Wilder remarked on its dual personality: "Either you motor sedately through a corner, or pressing on somewhat, you're herding an untamed beast, one which responds more to the throttle than to the wheel, and rather violently at that." *Road & Track* found a heavy-duty-sprung car much easier to control, and they put forth the conclusion that "it probably has more performance per dollar than anything you could buy."

The press predicted big changes for 1960—and for good reason. Bill Mitchell had been seen tooling around in a number of radically styled prototypes built on the Corvette chassis. Furthermore, some Chevy engineers had admitted to some disappointment in the 'Vette's fiberglass body. As *Sports Cars Illustrated* put it, "the extra beef built into the frame to compensate for lack of strength in the fiberglass structure takes away all the weight advantage." A steel unit-body, perhaps on a shorter wheelbase, could weigh 150 pounds less. The new, steel-bodied Corvette for 1960 would look like a cross between the Mitchell specials and a Ferrari 250 Testa Rossa. It would feature a rear-mounted transaxle and de Dion rear suspension. Extensive use of aluminum would lighten the engine, which with some modification could be bored out to over 400 cubic inches.

But the 1960 Corvette was nothing like that. Perhaps a little embarrassed by its own outlandish predictions, *SCI* blamed the compact, rear-engine Corvair for soaking up all of Chevy's engineering resources. That wasn't entirely true. In 1957, GM had planned an entirely new line of passenger cars, code-named "Q-cars," with aluminum engines, rear-mounted transaxles, and some sort of independent rear suspension, to be introduced in 1960. Duntov had laid out a small (94-inch wheelbase), lighter "Q-Corvette" chassis around these components, and Bob McLean, assisted by Bob Veryzer, Pete Brock, and John Bird, had sculpted a slim and graceful fastback body for it. At Mitchell's suggestion, McLean had borrowed the Q-Corvette's strong horizontal motif and prominent fender bulges from Boano's 1954-55 Abarth 207-A. It was the recession of 1958, not the Corvair, that had buried the project.

So the 1960 Corvette looked almost exactly like the '59 model, although aluminum heads did appear on the options list. These saved fifty-three pounds, and their superior heat conductivity allowed a compression ratio of 11.0:1. That, combined with larger intake valves and a larger plenum chamber, boosted horsepower of the top fuel-injected engine to 315 bhp.

Underneath, Duntov heeded the criticisms of the press and added a rear sway bar while fattening up the front bar even further. With these changes, he told the magazines, the standard-suspension Corvette could outhandle a '59 model with the heavy-duty springs. While admitting that this was probably true around town and on tight tracks, *SCI* questioned the usefulness of the rear

With its short, upturned tail borrowed from the XP-700, the 1961 model marked the beginning of Bill Mitchell's influence on the appearance of production Corvettes. It also provided a smooth transition to the more modern '63 Sting Ray and— along with the very similar '62 model—represented the final iteration of the original Corvette idea.

Top left: The elaborate, three-dimensional trunk badge, shown here on a 1961 model, hadn't changed since 1958. Top right: The 283-cubic-inch V8 appeared in a Corvette for the last time in 1961. The RPO 468 version, shown here, produced 270 bhp from two four-barrels and a high-performance camshaft—making it the most powerful carbureted engine offered in a Corvette that year. Bottom left: The 1961 Corvette instrument panel also dated from 1958. Quaint as it may look today, it at least grouped all of the dials in front of the driver—a change made at Duntov's behest. New for 1961 was a slimmer transmission tunnel, which allowed more foot room.

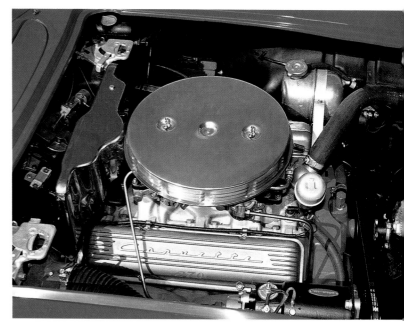

bar on long, fast courses, where the '60 Corvette occasionally lifted an inside rear wheel. Nonetheless, RPO 684 had disappeared from the options list.

The press can't be blamed for expecting more. The styling of the '53-'60 Corvettes—especially at the rear of the car—reflected a time that had gone by, when cars still sported bolt-on fenders whose forms were separate from the rest of the body. Indeed, the Corvette's trunk had been designed to be horizontally rounded because Earl originally wanted to put the spare tire on top of it! And by the late fifties, most other marques had outgrown their toothy grilles.

So 1961 brought at least a freshened front end with a simpler grille and less chrome, and an entirely new tail section lifted almost intact from Mitchell's ''experimental'' XP-700. ''This was a good move,'' commented *Road & Track*. ''There's no mistaking the Corvette for any other make and it is a better-looking car now.''

Under the skin, the Corvette remained substantially the same. The top engine option now featured iron heads with the same porting and compression ratio as the aluminum units that had dropped off the options list in March 1960. (Intricate casting of the recalcitrant high-silicon alloy had proven more difficult than anticipated, and the foundry found itself recycling far too many defective heads.) Gone too were the Cerametalix brakes, replaced by finned and fanned drums with air scoops in their backing plates.

Sports Cars Illustrated praised the '61 Corvette for its controllable handling but noted that the front brakes still faded under hard use. The magazine found the driving position improved as well: "No longer must the steering wheel be placed right under the chin." *Road & Track* agreed: "Most cars with riding qualities approaching those of the Corvette can't match its sticking ability on curves. And those that match or beat its handling usually ride like the proverbial truck." The close-ratio, four-speed transmission continued to win accolades from everyone who tried it, with *R&T* calling it "one of the best in the world."

For 1962, Cole and Barr increased the bore and stroke of the small-block V8 to 4 × 3¼ inches, for a displacement of 327 cubic inches. Corvette buyers could opt for one of four states of tune, from 250 bhp with a single four-barrel and 10.5:1 compression, all the way up to 360 bhp from 11.25:1 heads and fuel injection. Alterations to the grille and side trim gave the '62 Corvette an even bolder, cleaner look. But the most radical change in the history of the marque was yet to come.

Another view of the '61 Corvette. The styling cleanup included a simple mesh grille to replace the fearsome teeth of previous years. Painted (rather than chromed) headlight bezels and a simplified badge also helped turn down the glitter.

Right: *Corvette assembly in St. Louis, 1962. A workman installs the window mechanism and other body hardware on the trim line (top left). Later, the painted, sealed, and sanded body, complete with trim and hardware, joins the engine and chassis at the "body drop" (top right). After final inspection and clean-up (bottom), the new Corvette is ready to be driven off the line and into the garage of an appreciative owner. Opposite page: Corvette for 1962: the last of the solid-axle roadsters. This angle shows the harmony of smooth contours and sharp creases, demonstrating Bill Mitchell's genius for three-dimensional form. Under the hood, Chevrolet engineers enlarged the Corvette's V8 to 327 cubic inches, with horsepower ratings ranging from 250 bhp in base tune to 360 bhp with fuel injection.*

CHAPTER THREE

THE STING RAY, 1963-67

After I mounted that shark I caught at
Bimini, I kept looking at it on the wall,
and I said I'm going to make a car
look like that.
William L. Mitchell
From *Corvette: A Piece of the Action*

Bill Mitchell grew up, as he was fond of saying, with gasoline in his veins.

His father sold Buicks in Pennsylvania and never hesitated to soup up a tired old trade-in to boost its resale value. His mother lived in New York City, where Mitchell, on his fifteenth birthday, took a job as an office boy for the Collier Advertising Agency. Barron Collier's sons—who eventually would establish the Automobile Racing Club of America, an ancestor of the Sports Car Club of America—were about Bill's age, and he enjoyed racing home-built go-carts with them at the Collier family estate.

Less than a year out of high school, Bill became a layout artist and illustrator at Collier while studying nights at the Art Students' League. He still raced with the Colliers, who had graduated to real European sports cars and to a 5/8-mile dirt track in Tarrytown. A friend of a friend showed Mitchell's sketches to Harley Earl, and Mitchell, still in his early twenties, joined the GM styling staff in 1935.

Earl appointed Mitchell head of the Cadillac studio before he turned twenty-five. Bill designed some memorable cars for the division, notably the 60 Special of 1938, but sports cars remained his true love. He became assistant director of design for the corporation in 1950, and in December 1958 Earl picked Mitchell as his successor.

By the mid-fifties, Corvettes occasionally beat Jaguars and Mercedes in SCCA road races. Mitchell, who had once (unsuccessfully) requested a leave of absence to join the Mercedes-Benz Grand Prix team, asked Earl for permission to design and build a small series of Corvettes with bodies modified for road racing. These were the SR-2 Corvettes, marked by an extended nose, aerodynamic driver's headrest, and a single fin on the rear deck. Earl's son Jerry acquired a full-race version; another was built with a street chassis for Red Curtice.

Meanwhile, Zora Arkus-Duntov busied himself with a far more ambitious racing project: the magnesium-bodied, tube-framed Corvette SS, a prototype race car designed from the ground up to compete against Europe's best at Sebring and—if all went well there—Le Mans. Powered by a modified Corvette engine with aluminum heads and 307 bhp at 6400 rpm, the SS featured a ball-joint front suspension and a de Dion rear axle with inboard rear brakes, for significantly better handling than would have been possible with the stock Corvette chassis. Readied hastily for drivers John Fitch and Piero Taruffi at Sebring in 1957, it proved unbearably hot inside; and it suffered both brake and ignition problems before a broken suspension bushing finally took it out of the race.

Still, when it was running, the SS could pull out of the corners as fast as any Jaguar or Ferrari, and a thoroughly impressed Ed Cole told Duntov to go ahead and build three more cars for Le Mans. Then GM management decided that it wasn't going to finance any more auto racing. The reason became apparent in June, when the Automobile Manufacturer's Association (AMA) passed a resolution that "recommended" that member companies not participate in auto racing and that they "refrain from suggesting speed" in their advertising. The resolution had been proposed by Red Curtice. Chevrolet consigned the SS to storage.

Naturally, this disappointed racing-fan Mitchell, who spent nearly a year trying to figure out how to retrieve the SS project from the mothballs. Finally, he approached Ed

Opposite page, top left:
A pioneer in U.S. sportscar racing as well as automobile design, William L. Mitchell supervised the styling of all GM automobiles from 1959 through 1977. The Corvette, however, remained his favorite. This photo was taken close to his retirement in 1977. Top right: The Corvette SS, which Duntov designed specifically for European-style endurance racing. With its tubular space frame, magnesium body, and de Dion rear suspension, it differed considerably from any Corvette you could buy off the showroom floor. Trimmed as it is here, with a full-width windshield and the number 1, the SS challenged Europe's best at the 12 Hours of Sebring in 1957. The car delivered a strong performance but suffered from both brake and ignition problems before a broken suspension bushing finally took it out of the race. Bottom right: Duntov again with the SS. The removable canopy satisfied the closed-car rule in effect that year at some racing venues.

Cole and arranged to buy an incomplete SS test mule that Duntov had built to aid development of the actual race car. Mitchell would be allowed to race the car privately, providing he erased its Corvette identity.

Working in a secret studio with Californian Larry Shinoda, Mitchell transformed the Corvette SS into one of the most brilliant designs of his career. As fellow designer Strother MacMinn described it years later for *Automobile Quarterly*, the new body resembled ''an aerodynamically curved shingle barely passing over the wheels with tapered 'blips' for clearance.'' Although undeniably influenced by the same Boano fender line he had suggested for the Q-Corvette, Mitchell had deliberately avoided copying the look of the contemporary Ferrari or Jaguar or any other European make. ''By God, if it went to Le Mans,'' he said, ''I wanted everyone to know that this was an American car.'' Mitchell called his creation the Sting Ray, and he campaigned it in both SCCA and United States Auto Club (USAC) events in 1959 and 1960, usually with Dr. Thompson at the wheel.

GM's anti-racing stance had softened by 1959, however, and Duntov resumed his racing experiments, building a prototype single-seater largely out of Corvette SS components. The intolerably hot cockpit of the Corvette SS—and Duntov's positive experience with Porsches—inspired him to position the engine directly behind the driver. He named the car CERV-I, which stood for either Chevrolet Experimental Racing Vehicle or Chevrolet Engineering Research Vehicle, depending on the prevailing winds from the fourteenth floor. Its 96-inch wheelbase fit then-current rules for the Indianapolis 500. Duntov told GM management that a successful demonstration of CERV-I would dispel any public doubts about the rear-engine Corvair.

Of course, CERV-I existed because Duntov was contemplating a mid-engine Corvette. Cole backed this

Whose 'Vette Is It, Anyway?

Although Bill Mitchell technically oversaw the development of every production automobile designed at General Motors between 1958 and 1977, he always took a special, personal interest in the Corvette. Just how personal became apparent to Jean Lindamood, then an associate editor at *Car and Driver*, when she interviewed various members of the GM Design staff in March 1983.

Irv Rybicki, who had succeeded Mitchell as Design vice president, told Lindamood about the time he had launched his own Corvette project in 1960: "When Mitchell found out, he called me in and said, 'I wanna tell you something, kid. There's only one person in this organization who can design a Corvette, and that's *me*'." Designer Dave Holls also incurred Mitchell's wrath for merely *suggesting* a styling change for the 'Vette. "Don't flatter yourself, kid," Mitchell told him. "I do the 'Vettes in this building."

idea, but Mitchell's stylists did not; they had grown infatuated with the Boano/Q-Corvette/Sting Ray concept and wanted a new Corvette chassis to fit its emphatically front-engine proportions. And a front-engine chassis could save time and money by using more existing components. So in 1960, Duntov, Barr, and Premo began work on an all-new front-engine Corvette.

In December of that year, Duntov explained the evolution of the Corvette concept to *Sports Cars Illustrated*: ''Originally, our plan was to develop the car along separate touring and racing lines, as Jaguar did with the XK series on one hand and with the C-Type and D-Type on

the other. With this in mind we first introduced racing options, then the SR-2, finally the SS, which was intended to be our 'prototype' competition car. When this project was cut off, we realized we had to approach the Corvette in some other way.''

The only other way was to build both racing and touring capability into a single car. A long options list would help, but Duntov's elimination of the heavy-duty suspension in 1960 shows how serious he was about making one car do both jobs. One of his primary goals for the new car would be improved ride *and* improved handling. And for that he needed a new suspension.

In front, he made do with pieces lifted from the contemporary full-size Chevy—in fact, he had chosen the new 'Vette's shorter, 98-inch wheelbase as the shortest compatible with full-size Chevy components. This included ball joints at last, a feature big Chevrolets had enjoyed since 1955. Duntov tilted the upper wishbone arm back nine degrees to discourage brake dive.

If the front suspension design merely brought the 'Vette up to date, the rear suspension reached into the future. Borrowing from both CERV-I and contemporary (Formula 1) European road-racing technology, Duntov designed an independent suspension using fixed-length, double-jointed halfshafts as upper locating members—a system he believed superior to the de Dion setup of the SS and Sting Ray. The lower links angled downward from the differential casing to the wheel uprights, so that they were longer than the halfshafts and controlled the camber change as the body rolled, from 5.5 degrees negative at full compression to 4.0 degrees positive at full rebound. Stamped-steel trailing radius arms handled both driving and braking loads. The independent suspension reduced unsprung weight at the rear dramatically, from 350 to 210 pounds, and contributed to the goal of improved ride and handling. When the bean counters squealed about its cost, Duntov simply pointed to all the money he had saved by assembling the front suspension out of the Bel Air parts bin.

The new suspension also lowered the Corvette's rear roll center from 9.0 inches to 7.56. Since the new front suspension *raised* the roll center at that end by 3.4 inches, the entire car now rolled on a more nearly horizontal axis.

Duntov's choice of a nine-leaf transverse rear spring raised some eyebrows; no one had seen transverse leaf springs in a U.S. automobile since they had vanished from Ford's hopelessly obsolete line at the end of 1948.

Actually, as *Road & Track* pointed out, the Corvette setup more closely resembled that of the 1936-37 Cord, with the spring tied to the trailing links through rubber-cushioned tension struts. Chevrolet engineers argued the point that there was no place else to put a spring. (Jaguar used a similar suspension with two coils per side, but such complication would have been unthinkable in Detroit; CERV-I had made do with only a single coil per side, but it was a much lighter car, requiring much smaller springs.) And transverse leaf springs carry their own weight more effectively than any other automotive spring—which is the reason why Henry Ford had favored using them in the first place.

The engineers brought the steering up to date as well, discarding the archaic worm-and-sector gearbox for a modern recirculating-ball unit with an internal ratio of 16.0:1. The equally obsolescent center idler arm vanished to make way for modern three-link geometry with a hydraulic damper. Together with the ball-joint suspension, these changes allowed faster steering ratios with less effort. The steering arms came with two attachment points for the tie rods, so that a simple service operation could change the overall ratio from 19.6:1 to 17.0:1, that is from 3.4 turns lock-to-lock to 2.9. Another service operation could move the entire steering column 1.5 inches closer to or further from the driver. Power steering was offered for the first time, and *Car and Driver* said it was "every bit as good as those used by Rover and Mercedes-Benz in terms of feedback and road feel."

The full-size Chevy donated its brakes to the Corvette cause. At 2³/₄ inches wide in front, 2 inches wide in the rear, and 11 inches in diameter, they gave the 'Vette an 18-percent increase in lining area. A "Special Performance" option offered even bigger Al-Fin (finned aluminum) drums with segmented iron ("sintered metallic") linings, dual master cylinders (split front/rear) and a vac-

uum servo. The engineers had considered disc brakes and even installed a set of Dunlop discs on the original Sting Ray racer, but management vetoed them because of their cost.

Option Z06, available only on the coupe, deleted the steering damper and combined the Special Performance brakes and aluminum knock-off wheels with a heavy-duty suspension and a 36.5-gallon gas tank. (The latter pretty much took up the whole trunk.)

A new perimeter frame gave better rigidity without a central crossmember, permitted a lower seating position, and cleverly allowed the dual exhausts to pass through its lowest crossmember, the one below the seats. Interestingly, the original design called for a tube frame—light, stiff, but rather expensive. So, one by one, the engineers replaced the tubes with box-section members, trading weight for cost, until no tubular members at all reached production. Still, at 260 pounds, the new frame weighed no more than the old one and provided 50 percent more torsional stiffness. The body bolted down to this frame at six points in each of the steel door-sill reinforcements, uniting body and chassis in a single rigid unit.

The old Corvette had been balanced for understeer, with 53 percent of its curb weight on its front wheels; now, Duntov shifted both the engine and the seats even further back, so that 52 percent of the Corvette's weight rode on its rear tires—a situation he considered more suited for a high-performance car. Reflecting this change, standard spring rates were now set at 105 pounds per inch in front, 125 pounds per inch in the rear.

Reliable horsepower and sophisticated handling made the '63 Corvette a natural for road racing. Sting Rays won the SCCA's B-Production national championship in 1963, and many individual cars, like this '63 roadster, continued to compete into the seventies and eighties.

The 327-cubic-inch V8 introduced in 1962 remained fundamentally the same, still available in 250-, 300-, 340-, and 360-bhp editions. Although already labeled an anachronism by the press, the three-speed manual transmission survived as base equipment with all four engines; but all four could be ordered with a four-speed, which had a taller, 2.20:1 first gear on the 340- and 360-bhp cars. An alternator replaced the generator, the flywheel got smaller (so the engine could mount lower), and the intake plenum on the injected version again got bigger.

Powerglide could be ordered with only the two lower-output engines. The options sheet also boasted a whopping six different axle rations, from 3.36 (standard with either three-speed or Powerglide), to 3.70 (standard with four-speed), then 3.08, 3.55, 4.11, and 4.56. Interestingly, the engineers offset the entire driveline one inch to the right to give the driver more footroom.

A full-size clay model completed in October 1959 clearly established the theme of the new body: essentially the racing Sting Ray with the Q-Corvette's teardrop-shaped greenhouse grafted on top. Since the Sting Ray was derived from the Q-Corvette anyway, the final effect was more harmonious than it sounded. A central ridge split the rear window in two.

Duntov objected. How could the driver see out? "If you take that off, you might as well forget the whole thing," huffed Mitchell. A master salesman, he knew how to make management see things his way. The rear window remained split, and a second clay model, presented to management in April 1960, resembled the definitive '63 Corvette in all but a few details. On Christmas Eve 1961, Mitchell won the approval he sought for the final design.

Ed Cole wanted a 2+2 version to follow the two-seater a year later. This time Mitchell objected, and so

did Barr, and Cole relented. But in the meantime, the stylists had raised the Corvette's windshield high enough to allow for an extended roofline. The press loved the extra headroom, but Mitchell wrote later that because of this compromise the '63 Corvette "looked stocky as hell."

GM designer Dr. Peter Kryopoulos tested 3/8 scale models in the Cal Tech wind tunnel, looking for an ideal compromise between appearance and aerodynamics. Chevrolet released no drag numbers, saying only that the new coupe had less total air drag than the old roadster with the hard top on, and a lower drag coefficient than the racing Sting Ray's unimpressive 0.44. Duntov wasn't satisfied with the results, but of course he said nothing publicly at the time. Years later, he admitted to *Car and Driver* that at high speed the '63-'67 Corvette body developed "just enough lift to be a bad airplane."

Chevrolet claimed that the Corvette's concealed headlights resulted from aerodynamic experiments as well, and that this styling fillip also kept the lights safe from dirt and stones during daylight driving. If necessary, they could be rotated manually by cranks under the hood.

The coupe body carried steel reinforcements around the doors and under the cowl, so despite its smaller

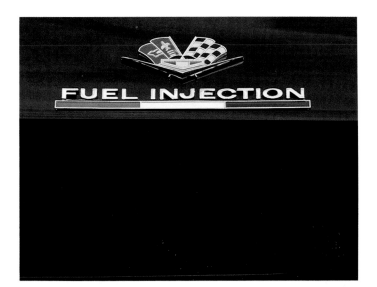

dimensions, it weighed more than the previous body. Curved side glass and cowl-top ventilation brought the Corvette into the sixties. Chevrolet claimed that the heater was better too, and that the new trunk offered more usable space—even if there was no external lid. (The spare tire lived in a fiberglass tub that hinged downward from the rear of the car.) Combined with the smaller chassis, the 1963 Corvette weighed 34 to 50 pounds less than its immediate ancestor.

In spite of their disagreements, both Mitchell and Duntov had at last created the Corvette they wanted. They had so totally transformed the car that in October 1962 *Road & Track* commented that all the changes that had come before amounted to only "a few minor details" in comparison. "The 1963 Corvette has come a long way in 10 years," the editors concluded, "from a stylists' plaything to a full-blown, out-and-out dual-purpose sports car." Even the name was new: officially, all Corvettes were now Sting Rays.

And at just 49.5 inches tall, even the new coupe stood 2.5 inches lower than the old roadster—with the top down. The grilles on the hood were dummies, of course (otherwise they would have spewed engine fumes into the cowl vents right behind them), but as *Car and Driver* pointed out, "if it turns out that aerodynamic lift at racing speeds is a problem, making them genuine with a hacksaw would be easy." Duntov told *Car and Driver* that the coupe, in full street trim, could reach 155 mph, and the convertible 150. "For the first time I now have a Corvette I can be proud to drive in Europe," he told *C/D*. "We understand his feelings," added the editors, "and are happy to agree that the Sting Ray is a fine showpiece for the American auto industry."

"In most ways it's as advanced as the latest dual-purpose sports/luxury cars from Europe," wrote Roger Huntington in *Motor Trend*, "—and this includes the new

Jaguar XK-E, Ferrari GT, Mercedes 300-SL, and all the rest." *MT* measured 130 mph on the back stretch of Riverside Raceway, driving a 360-bhp car with 3.70 rear.

The St. Louis plant doubled its production schedule, and still most Chevy dealers had waiting lists of at least 60 days for the new car. And they weren't discounting the price, either. Still, some flaws emerged when *Car and Driver* tested a 300-bhp example (the most popular engine option) in April 1963. The extreme roll stiffness built into the independent suspension limited its benefits on rough pavement, where the testers found it "veering freely from one course to another, making high-frequency corrections s.o.p. [standard operating procedure]." Interestingly, the entire staff preferred to keep the steering wheel in its most distant position.

But with a new Corvette in production, the press also seemed less gently disposed toward the old one. "The early Corvette did a wonderful job in competition against all-out sports/racing cars," wrote Huntington in the January '63 *Motor Trend*, "but its handling couldn't be described as 'modern' or 'advanced' in any sense of the words.... You could wrestle it around a corner, but it wasn't an easy car to drive fast."

"That production component live rear axle," *Road & Track* admitted in October 1962, "could hop and dance like an Apache with a hot foot." The Sting Ray's independent rear made all the difference: "Whether you slam the car through an S-bend at 85 or pop the clutch at 5000 rpm at the drag strip, the result is the same—great gripping gobs of traction." Compared to the old Corvette, the Sting Ray put more power into accelerating, less into obliterating its own tires. *Road & Track* noted that the '63 360-bhp car they tested, which was equipped with a 3.70:1 differential, actually equalled the 0-60 times recorded by *Car Life* for a '62 360-bhp 'Vette with a (live) 4.11:1 axle!

Opposite page, top and bottom: With the debut of the split-window coupe in 1963, the Corvette was offered for the first time with two different body styles. Still, roadsters continued to outsell coupes through 1968. The fender logo on the roadster shown here indicates that it featured the 340-bhp fuel-injected engine. The cast-aluminum knock-off wheels on the coupe are the subject of some controversy: while they appeared on 1963 option sheets—and were even listed as part of the Z06 package— many historians believe that problems with porous castings delayed their actual introduction until 1964.

Improvements were not limited to a better grip on the pavement. "One thing the designers thought of this time around," *Road & Track* quipped, "[is] the driver." More room, better seats, a better instrument layout, a lockable glove box, and the adjustable steering column made the Corvette better suited to human habitation. "Our only complaint about the interior was in the coupe," wrote the editors, "where all we could see in the rear-view mirror was that silly bar splitting the window down the middle." *Motor Trend* technical editor Jim Wright also noted that "any decent view to the rear will have to be through an exterior side-view mirror." He added that the brushed-aluminum instrument faces made the gauges hard to read at night.

Opinion divided sharply over quality control. *Motor Trend*'s Wright complained about ripply fiberglass and cheap interior moldings; *Road & Track* consistently defended Corvette quality as "first rate."

In any case, the split window only lasted one year in production, and when it vanished in 1964, no one seemed to miss it. *Motor Trend* called the change "a safety factor," but fussed more over the '64 'Vette's new variable-rate springs, which was another idea that Duntov had developed on the Corvette SS and CERV-I. A new forced-air ventilation system used an electric fan that was stashed in the left rear quarter panel to suck hot air out of the luggage compartment. "Some of last year's gingerbread is missing," *MT* noted, and indeed it was true that the bogus hood grilles and shiny instrument faces had vanished along with the split window.

Handsome aluminum knock-off wheels, announced in '63 but delayed because of porous castings, finally appeared on production Corvettes. But the adapters needed to connect them to the Corvette's five-bolt hubs offset any weight saving that the aluminum alloy might have provided.

At the same time, new camshafts and intake manifolds upped the output of the 340-bhp engine to 360, and a new cam took the fuel-injected 360 to 375. Testing a "fuelie" with a 4.11 rear at Riverside, *Motor Trend* assistant technical editor Bob McVay blasted through the quarter-mile in only 14.2 seconds at an honest 100 mph. On the back straight, he wrote, "our black coupe whistled right up to 134 mph as the tachometer needle touched the 6700-rpm red line." McVay praised the 'Vette's gearbox as "one of the best we've tested," described the stopping power of its heavy-duty brakes as "amazing," and concluded that "not only was the Sting Ray a fine-handling automobile on the race course, it also proved a very comfortable and refined sports tourer."

Road & Track deliberately selected a tamer Corvette for its test that year, a 300-bhp model with power steering and automatic transmission, but arrived at a remarkably similar conclusion: "an ideal fast tourer for those who are not interested in the ultimate in performance." The automatic car still zipped through the quarter mile in only 15.2 seconds. And with its quick 17.6:1 ratio and only 2.92 turns lock-to-lock, they found the 'Vette's power steering "one of the best we have ever encountered...fast, responsive and effortless...."

For 1965, the stylists excised a few more of the car's original excesses. With the hood grilles gone, there was no reason to keep the indentations where they had been, so these disappeared as well, leaving just a smooth surface with a subtle central hump. And the fake vents behind the front wheels became real air outlets: three bold gashes in the side of the car, like shark gills. Some magazines applauded these changes, but *Road & Track* didn't think they'd gone far enough. "It has enough pizzazz for a movie set," the editors moaned in December 1964, "or [for] nymphet nabbing, or for the types who get their jollies from looking at all that glitter."

More important, the Corvette finally arrived with disc brakes—11¾-inch vented discs on all four wheels, no less. These increased the Corvette's total swept brake area from 321 to 461.2 square inches. (Apparently trying to use up its inventory of brake drums, GM offered the old brakes as a "credit option.") *Road & Track* praised the new disc-type binders not only for their effective stopping power but for feel and feedback as well.

The three-speed transmission now came with the 250-bhp engine only: four-speeds were standard with other power plants. Among those other mills was a new 350-bhp 327 with 11.0:1 compression and hydraulic lifters. It was one of these that *Car and Driver* tested for April 1965, and it scooted through the quarter mile in 14.9 seconds with a 3.36 rear. This inspired *C/D*'s pundits to pen a witty review explaining why "the best 'Vette yet," in

spite of its world-class ride, handling, acceleration, interior comfort, and so on, would *never* be the equal of the Aston Martin or Ferrari. The underlying message, if you read beneath the sarcasm, was that it already was.

Rumors flew about a new, bigger engine for the Corvette. Chevrolet had recently introduced a 396-cubic-inch version of its 427-cubic-inch NASCAR (National Association for Stock Car Racing) engine to replace the optional 409-cubic-inch big block in its full-size cars. In the fall of 1964, Chevrolet applied to SCCA to homologate a 396-cubic-inch Corvette in the production category. The car didn't actually appear until fairly late in the model year, however, long after SCCA had removed it from its "approved" list.

Still, the first big-block Corvette left a lasting impression. The engine itself featured the "porcupine heads"

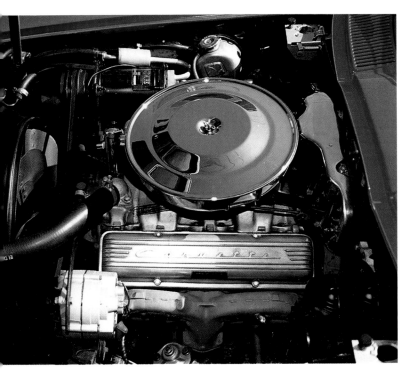

of the NASCAR 427, with the intake and exhaust valves angled away from each other in both the transverse and longitudinal planes. Compared to the old 409, it boasted about 12 percent more bearing area, with stronger four-bolt rather than two-bolt mains. And at 680 pounds, it weighed a good 80 pounds more than the small-block 327—but it produced a whopping 425 bhp at 6400 rpm.

A louvered blister on the top of the hood distinguished 396-powered Corvettes from their 327 siblings. To accommodate the bigger engine, the Corvette also needed a bigger antiroll bar up front—which in turn necessitated an antiroll bar in the rear. A wider radiator, bigger fan, stronger half-shafts and U-joints, and, of course, a stiffer clutch completed the package.

Road & Track cursed that stiff clutch, which proved extremely nonlinear just for good measure. Wheel spin

Above: The Sting Ray roadster for 1965. Only 759 Corvettes were built with the factory side-mounted exhaust. This example also features the relatively rare cast-aluminum knock-off wheels. Left: Corvette engines for 1965 ranged from a basic 250-bhp small-block to the thundering 425-bhp 396. This car's mid-range L79 327 produced 350 bhp from a single four-barrel carburetor and 11.0:1 compression.

was a problem for the first time in a Sting Ray, limiting quarter-mile times to 14.1 seconds with the 3.70 rear—about what the fuel-injected car could do with a 4.11. "It is not a car for the inexpert or the inattentive," wrote *R&T*'s editors. "On anything except dead dry paving, the car is going to be a very large handful." Even with all that horsepower, they questioned whether the big-block Corvette could beat the lighter (by 800 pounds), wider-tired Cobra around a road course.

General Motors didn't see it that way. The expensive fuel-injection option quietly vanished in 1966, while the 396 grew to its full NASCAR displacement of 427 cubic inches. Even Duntov admitted later that cubic inches produced horsepower more cheaply than fuel injection. Chevrolet still rated the hot, solid-lifter edition at 425 bhp, and introduced a new, hydraulic-lifter version with

lower (10.25:1 compression), smaller ports, milder cam, and 390 bhp.

When *Car and Driver* asked Duntov why power hadn't increased with displacement, he slyly replied that "you must remember that cast iron is very heavy, and by removing thirty cubic inches of it, we have made a significant reduction in weight." In truth, the extra cubes boosted rated torque from 415 pound-feet at 4000 rpm to 465—and Chevrolet probably preferred that the insurance companies not know just how much horsepower the engine really made. In the same article, *C/D* suggested that the 396 probably had produced more than 425 gross horsepower as well.

At the same time, the 300-bhp 327 became the standard power plant, with the 350-horse 327 optional. Chevrolet discontinued the forced-air ventilation system—it had never worked well, anyway—so the louvers vanished from the coupe's roof pillars. Aside from that, only an egg-crate grille and some revised badging distinguished the '66 Corvette from the '65.

After testing a 427 Corvette in November 1965, *Car and Driver* suggested that the big-block car had lost something in the translation. Gone was the "zippy, high-winding, no-flywheel feel" that had characterized all V8 Corvettes (but especially the fuel-injected models) since 1955. In its place were "great gobs of steam-locomotive, earth-moving torque…that overwhelms every other sensation." Still, with power steering that was "superior to any other American car…the extra weight of this big engine doesn't really seem to affect the car's handling at all…. When you're going fast it's quick and responsive… and it'll hold its own in any company at any price." Corvette sales reached a new model-year high of 22,940.

The press expected all-new styling for 1967, and only in July of 1966 did *Motor Trend* finally admit that this was "impossible." At the same time, *MT* predicted a minor face-lift for 1967, a major one for '69—and an all-new, *mid-engine* Corvette in 1971.

Instead, the '67 Corvette differed from the '66 only in details. Four shark fins now interrupted the front fenders, instead of three, and these were blended together to form a single rectangular unit. The rear end sported a huge single reverse light at its center. *Road & Track* called the 'Vette's new look "purposeful, almost elegant…it finally looks the way we thought it should have in the first place." The parking brake migrated to the center console, and bolt-on alloy wheels that really did save weight replaced the heavy knock-offs.

Even the awkward big-block hood bulge evolved into a handsome simulated scoop. Underneath lurked one of three different 427s—a 390-bhp version essentially identical to the previous year's; a 400-bhp edition with three

two-barrel Holleys; and a solid-lifter, triple-carburetor fire-breather rated 435 bhp. Of course, only the insurance underwriters were supposed to believe those numbers. The triple-carb setup featured 1.50-inch primaries in the center and 1.75-inch secondaries at the ends. Interestingly, the throttle linkage connected only to the center carburetor; the secondaries were controlled by vacuum lines from the primary venturis. For the first time, Chevrolet offered Powerglide with either of the hydraulic-lifter big blocks—but not with the 350-bhp 327.

Motor Trend ushered a 435-bhp 'Vette with a 3.55 rear through the quarter-mile in 13.8 seconds at 104 mph, and called it "easily the most powerful production car made." *Car and Driver* obtained similar results (13.6 seconds and 105 mph) from a similar car, and remarked that the vacuum carburetor linkage "results in an astoundingly tractable engine and uncannily smooth engine response….On the whole, the Corvette's three deuces are as smooth and responsive as fuel injection." The *C/D* test car was an L89 version with aluminum heads and

Corvette instrument faces changed again in 1965, abandoning the recessed center cones that had been finished in bright aluminum in 1963 and in black in 1964. At last, the gauges acquired a more business-like look, which remains unchanged on this example from 1966.

Right: The last of the Sting Rays proved the cleanest of all; even the traditional crossed-flag emblem was left off the front fenders. The most distinctive feature of the '67 'Vette was its new front-fender air outlet, which now consisted of four louvers integrated into a single, rectangular opening. New standard equipment included 6-inch, styled steel "Rally Wheels," which replaced the plain 5½-inch steel wheel and wheel cover offered previously. Opposite page, top left: New seats arrived in 1967, but the instrument cluster remained unchanged since 1965. Middle left: Even the fuel filler was simplified for 1967. Bottom left: The attractive "Stinger" hood scoop allowed room for big-block engines in 1967, replacing the louvered bulge of 1965–66. Top right: The triple carburetor option was new in 1967. Bottom right: Just as pretty as the '67 roadster on the previous page is the Sting Ray coupe for '67.

larger valves; the engine weighed seventy-five pounds less than an all-iron 427 and only forty pounds more than a 327. Duntov himself had suggested to the editors that they try this particular engine.

But wait—even that wasn't the top of the engine line. Spring brought the L88, with 12.5:1 aluminum heads and a single, enormous four-barrel linked directly to a cowl induction flap at the rear of the hood scoop. (The air cleaner was built into the hood and lifted up with it.) Chevrolet blueprinted all L88 engines at the factory—to spare potential racers the trouble—but still coyly advertised only 435 bhp. L88 owners had to add aftermarket headers to realize this engine's full potential, but its real output, right out of the box, was closer to 560 bhp. L88 Corvettes were pure race cars, and to discourage poseurs from driving them on the street, Duntov arranged that they could not be ordered with radios or heaters.

Road & Track tried a milder, 327-cid/300-bhp car with the 3.36 final, which could still turn the quarter in sixteen seconds flat. "The Corvette ranks with the best sports/GT cars the world has to offer," wrote the testers, "regardless of price." The Corvette offered a unique combination of performance with smoothness, flexibility, and even economy (14-18 mpg isn't bad for 300 bhp, even today). But after five years of production, time was catching up with the Sting Ray. The suspension that had so impressed *R&T* back in 1963 was by 1967 "no match for the best European examples, like the Mercedes 230 SL or BMW 2000 CS." *Car and Driver* complained about heavy, numb steering and a stiff, uncommunicative ride. *R&T* noted that a new Corvette was coming, and wished for "lighter weight, improved body structure and quality control, and a better ride on poor surfaces."

Chevrolet had something else in mind.

CHAPTER FOUR

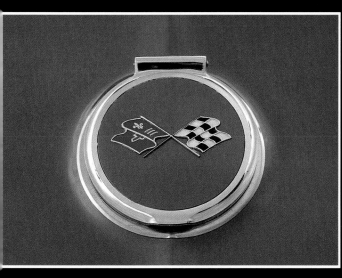

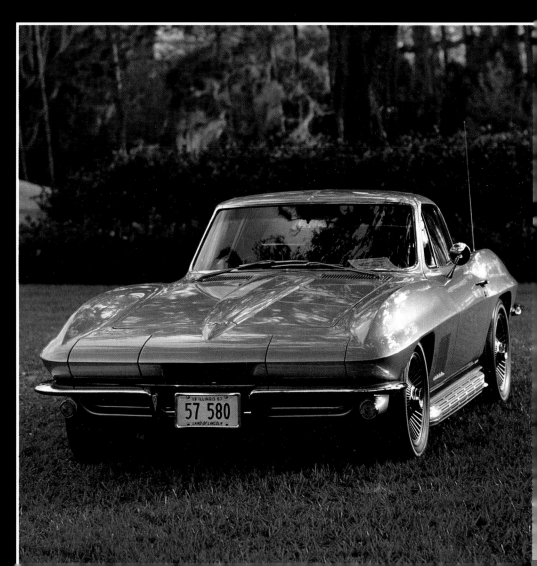

PEAKS AND VALLEYS, 1968-75

*It was an axiom of the soaring, sporty
sixties in the American automobile
business that no matter how good
your car was one year, you had
to change it for the next year, even
if you made it worse.*
Karl Ludvigsen
From *Corvette: America's
Star-Spangled Sports Car*

Bill Mitchell was still admiring the shark mounted on his wall.

It was the fall of 1962. St. Louis was bolting together Sting Rays as fast as the suppliers could deliver the parts. But new cars—even spectacular new cars—grew stale quickly in those days of planned obsolescence. Mitchell knew he needed to plan the *next* Corvette.

He took another look at that fish.

Then he described the car he wanted to Larry Shinoda: it would retain the boattail roofline of the production Sting Ray, but little else. The wheels were to be emphasized even more, with fenders that stood out prominently from a pinched-in cockpit. The beltline was to be lower, so that the roof blended into the upper body. And it would be painted to look like that shark: dark blue at the top, fading to light gray at the rocker panels.

In March 1965, Shinoda's crew rolled the outrageous Mako Shark outside for publicity photos. The car debuted publicly one month later at the New York Auto Show. By then it had been renamed the Mako Shark II, to distinguish it from the Shark, an earlier, similarly painted idea car Mitchell had based on the Sting Ray. A spread on the Mako Shark in *Motor Trend* let the pictures do most of the talking but commented that the show car featured the ''same general shape, and the same wicked look'' as its predatory namesake.

Duntov still hoped for a mid-engine Corvette, built on a Porschesque steel platform and incorporating a built-in steel roll bar, at least in the coupe. But such a car would require too many components not shared with other GM products. And it did not bode well for unconventional drivelines when new Chevrolet general manager Elliot ''Pete'' Estes halted development of the Corvair in the spring of 1965.

Of course, it just happened that Shinoda had also designed a mass-producible version of the Mako Shark II. Designers David Holls and Henry Haga further developed Shinoda's Mako Shark into a production-ready automobile. By the fall, they had a prototype on the Milford proving ground. But as troublesome as the Sting Ray had proven, aerodynamically, the Shark was worse. Furthermore, its peaky front fenders and heavy roofline blocked vision out of the cockpit. Duntov convinced Estes to delay the new car one model year—from 1967 to 1968—so that these problems could be addressed. Shinoda himself helped in the revisions, reshaping the car's fenders and tail section without compromising its theme.

The new Corvette that finally appeared in the fall of 1967 was breathtaking to look at—seven inches longer, half an inch narrower, and two inches lower than the Sting Ray. The height reduction was quite an accomplishment, since it rode atop the same chassis. Among the Shark's most notable features were roof panels that lifted off (an idea pioneered on the Q-Corvette) and a flat rear window that lifted out, essentially converting the coupe into an open car. Duntov got his roll bar, although it had to be braced with a T-bar against the windshield. Chevrolet still offered a traditional roadster as well, with both hard and soft tops.

The designers now lifted some styling features of the Mako Shark II almost intact. Vacuum-powered headlights popped up from the 'Vette's long nose, and another vacuum-powered panel of die-cast aluminum hid the windshield wipers. They even camouflaged the

door handles, blending a recessed finger-grip into the top edge of the door and leaving only the lock button showing from the side. The Sting Ray designation vanished along with the distinctive look that had defined it; the new car was, at least for the time being, simply a Corvette. And despite its elaborate shape, the new Corvette bowed as clean and unadorned as the Sting Ray had been overdecorated.

Still, the Mako Shark-based 'Vette lacked the Sting Ray's stunning originality. Jonathan Thompson—for decades *Road & Track*'s resident styling critic—praised the new Corvette for "basic surfaces [that] are far cleaner than the Sting Ray's," but went on to criticize it as "an assemblage of independent styling clichés" from other cars ranging from the '64 Ferrari 250 GTO to Chevrolet's own Camaro—including the latter's truly awful rocker-panel treatment. "True advances in automotive styling are made," wrote Thompson, "when a

new chassis or component grouping demands a really fresh solution to surface form....making a car 7.0 inches longer on an existing chassis is an unacceptable, easy-way-out solution to market stimulation."

Motor Trend, on the other hand, liked the "blood-stirring" new styling just fine. "The Picassoesque multiple-visage sculpturing, achieved with bumps and humps of old, has given way to a more harmonious, flowing theme that, in our opinion, is clearly a refinement over that of the previous model," wrote the editors in October 1967. In February, they named the new Corvette Sports Car of the Year. *Car and Driver* called it "the wildest-looking production car Detroit has ever made."

The aggressive-looking new dashboard also had been lifted almost intact from the Mako Shark II, but by 1968 the shape already had been seen on both the Camaro and the Corvair. It featured an enormous hood and two huge instrument pods situated directly in front of the driver. In the Corvette, these housed the speedometer and tachometer; the clock and gauges for water temperature, oil pressure, voltage, and fuel level moved to the center of the dash. *Road & Track* agreed that aesthetically, at least, this represented an improvement over the twin-arch dash of the old Sting Ray.

The Sting Ray's vertical console had evolved into a more modern, horizontal unit. Dash-level air vents enhanced interior comfort, and exit vents on the rear deck, just behind the window, provided Astro-Ventilation, which in *R&T*'s opinion still didn't work very well. A new seat-belt warning light had to be deactivated by a push switch after you buckled up. (Of course, it didn't know if you *had* buckled up!) An interesting innovation was the fiber-optic system that monitored all external lights (even the license-plate light) except for the side markers. These, like the Corvette's new collapsible steering column, had been mandated recently by the U.S. federal government.

Road & Track welcomed the greater clearance between the driver's belt buckle and the steering wheel (the latter

still adjusted through a three-inch range) but complained about mediocre seats; *Car and Driver* groused about tight shoulder room. And with its flat deck and tunneled backlight, the new body cut interior storage space radically. Even the new convertible lost what precious little trunk space it once had. With its fenders trimmed per Duntov's suggestion, the new body offered better forward vision than the old one—thanks mainly to its lower cowl—but vision to the rear had gotten even worse.

Changes under the skin were limited. Duntov relocated the inboard mounting point of the lower suspension arms, lowering the roll center to 4.71 inches and improving steering response. At the same time, his engineers specified new nominal rates for the progressive front springs: 80 pounds per inch for 327s, 92 pounds per inch for big-blocks. Duntov told *Road & Track* that these changes maintained the same total roll stiffness while biasing the chassis slightly toward understeer—a change made necessary, he said, by the power oversteer available from the seven-liter engine. Even so, big-block

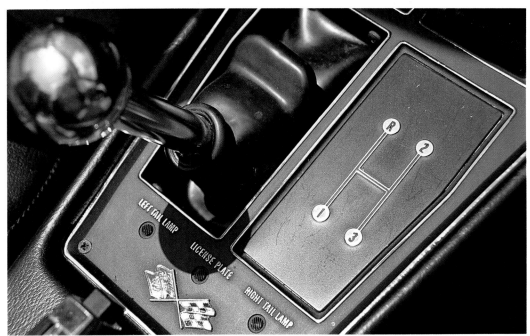

'Vettes still packed a bigger front antiroll bar (.9375 versus .7500 inches on '68 small-blocks), and used a .562-inch bar in the rear, where small blocks still got by on the inherent roll stiffness of the transverse rear spring. Distribution of roll couple—that is, the relative roll stiffness of the front and rear suspensions—was now 53/47 on 327s, 52/48 on 427s.

The engineers widened the track by 0.7 inches to 58.3 inches in front and 59.0 in the rear, and widened the wheels to 7 x 15. All of this added up to an even harsher ride than before—but that, said *Road & Track*, was "the price of making a brute-power, heavy car stick to the road when the driver decides to put his foot in it."

The disc brakes introduced in 1965 remained unchanged, as did the linkage-assisted power steering, and the engine choices, small and large. But Chevrolet finally laid the old Powerglide transmission to rest, replacing it with a three-speed Turbo Hydra-Matic. The new body dictated a lower cross-flow radiator, with its head tank on the right side, and the battery migrated to a compartment behind the seats—less for weight distribution than to save space under the hood.

Road & Track sampled a 400-bhp 'Vette in October 1967, and criticized it harshly for its stiff ride and heavy, numb steering. "There are few places today where one can make full use of such brute machinery," wrote one tester, while the "light-hearted responsiveness" of a European sports car "can be enjoyed every day." And the 'Vette's new interior, with its myriad warning lights, smacked of "Thunderbirdery." On the other hand, the big engine proved smoother than expected, and the Turbo Hydra-Matic "worked beautifully."

R&T tried two more 'Vettes for the January issue. The first was a triple-carb, 435-bhp model that tended to overheat both itself and its passengers. "Everything has been sacrificed to one cause," concluded the editors:

"Blinding acceleration....If you intend to use your Corvette as transportation, try another combination."

The *R&T* testers took their own advice and tried a Corvette roadster with the 350-bhp 327. With a 3.70 rear, this car sprinted through the quarter mile in 15.6 seconds at 92 mph—measurably slower than a similarly equipped Sting Ray. The testers enjoyed the 'Vette's superb Muncie gearbox, but they claimed that the power assists for both steering and brakes, as well as the rough-road ride, no longer matched the best from Europe. Worse still, the Corvette showed signs of hasty assembly: the clutch linkage rubbed against electrical wires, causing a short; the wiper cover wouldn't close; and upon close inspection the fiberglass body looked ripply and dull.

Writing in the December 1967 issue of *Car and Driver*, Steve Smith complained of poorly fitted body panels and a plethora of minor hardware failures—such as door locks that wouldn't lock, ashtrays that wouldn't pull out, knobs that fell off the dashboard, and windshield wipers that collided together "with a resounding crash." It was so bad that *C/D* elected to postpone its Corvette test until a later issue. To be fair, however, Smith pointed out that quality control on *all* Detroit products had been declining since the early sixties, as management pushed for faster and faster production.

When *C/D* did get around to testing a 427 coupe in May, the editors called the new Corvette "the best yet.... it's the only fiberglass-bodied, independently suspended, V8-powered, 4-wheel disc braked production car in the world...When you consider that it can be had for less than $6000 we can't think of a better deal." The 400-bhp beast blasted through the quarter in 14.1 seconds at 102 mph, despite a somewhat unpredictable response from the vacuum-operated secondaries. *C/D* concluded that little besides the Corvette's appearance had changed from the '63–'67 Sting Ray: the transmission was still terrific, the ride still harsh. The new roll-stiffness bias forced the driver to use power in turns to avoid "grinding off the front tires," but the wider wheels and lower center of gravity had definitely raised the car's cornering limits. And despite the engine heat and loss of width, they found the 'Vette "an outstandingly comfortable car to drive....It's

The stunningly different '68 Corvette bowed to reviews ranging from "blood-stirring" to "cliché." Undeniably cleaner than the '63 Sting Ray, the '68 'Vette carried its predecessor's marine-predator theme to its streetable extreme. Sales surged in 1969, slumped in 1970, but then rose steadily for most of the rest of this generation's fifteen-year life span.

Right: The '69 Corvette looked nearly identical to the '68, but packed a larger standard engine—now 350 cubic inches—wider wheels, and a host of technical improvements. Sales jumped 35 percent, and for the first time in Corvette history, coupes outsold roadsters. Opposite page, top left: The Stingray name returned in 1969, albeit now merged into one word. Chrome liners for the fender vents, available that year only, proved a popular option; nearly one Corvette in three that year left the factory so equipped. But just one buyer in nine opted for the side-mounted exhaust. Top right: This front view of a '69 Stingray clearly shows the more modest hood bulge supplied with small-block engines. Bottom: Radical fender contours, a narrow cockpit, and a deeply tunneled backlight characterize the new Corvette generation that began in 1968. Eight-inch-wide wheels were new for 1969, the year this coupe was built.

American and no other description begins to capture it.... The Corvette is a brilliant car with all of the virtues and all of the vices of American technology.'' Sales for the model year reached a healthy 28,566.

But by the spring of 1968, Chevrolet publicity had launched a campaign to forever confuse and confound automotive historians. They started to call the new Corvette a Sting Ray. The revival became official in the fall, when 1969 Corvettes began rolling off the line with chrome script reading STINGRAY—now one word—above the shark gills on their front fenders.

Around the same time, Chevrolet engineers were working with Bartz Engine Development in Van Nuys, California, on an all-aluminum edition of the L88 427. Set up for racing with Lucas/Crower fuel injection, this exotic power plant pulled anywhere from 590 to 615 horsepower (depending on ram-tube length) on Bartz's dyno, and reportedly weighed forty pounds less than an

all-iron 327. *Motor Trend*'s cover for September 1968 asked, bluntly, ''Is Ford dead?''

Perhaps not. But by December, *MT* reported that the 620-bhp aluminum V8 would be offered in the Stingray —as a $3000 option. The editors predicted an 11-second, 130-mph quarter mile. Ultimately, Chevrolet sold only two Corvettes (but perhaps as many as sixty-nine Camaros) with this all-aluminum engine.

More important, Chevrolet had taken the various criticisms of the '68 'Vette seriously and had significantly improved the '69 model, making such adjustments as stiffening the frame, adding a storage pouch to the dashboard where the glove box wasn't, and improving the door latches and the Astro-Ventilation (which, according to *Road & Track*, still provided almost no ventilation at all). More significant, the division replaced the Corvette's 300- and 350-bhp 327s with new 350-cubic-inch V8s. These were essentially 327s with another 15/64 inch

Opposite page, top: *Flared fenders introduced in 1970 not only looked racy but also kept stones thrown by the tires from damaging the sides of the car—a real problem on '68–'69 models. Air-outlet grating on the front fenders matched the grid texture of the all-new front grille, while interior options now included real leather seats and fake wood trim. Opposite page, bottom: To offset the power-dampening effects of government-mandated emission controls, Chevrolet lengthened the big block's stroke from 3⁴⁹/₆₄ inches to a full 4 inches, resulting in a displacement of 454 cubic inches, the biggest of any Chevy engine ever built for a street vehicle.*

of stroke. Still rated 300 and 350 bhp, they both produced 380 pound-feet of torque against the 327's 360. Chevrolet announced a 370-bhp 350, but this did not actually materialize until the following year.

Larger, eight-inch-wide wheels complemented the torquier engines, and the brake servo was recalibrated for better feedback. *Road & Track* again chose a triple-carb 427 for its test car, and again complained about the 'Vette's harsh ride and skittish handling over less-than-perfect pavement. Still, the testers liked "the delightfully light and positive" shifter and the surprisingly light clutch, praised the big block for its flexibility (it turned a 14.3-second quarter mile at 98 mph with a 4.11 rear), and allowed that on smooth roads, at least, "the Corvette is one of the best-handling front-engine production cars in the world." Coupes outsold convertibles for the first time, 22,129 to 16,633.

An article in the September 1969 *Car and Driver* attempted to sum up the Corvette dichotomy. "The small-engine Corvettes are marginally fast and extraordinarily civilized," wrote the editors, with some poetic license, while "the large-engine Corvettes are extraordinarily fast and marginally civilized." Sports car *cognoscenti*, wrote the editors, would never accept the 'Vette because of its mass-produced origin in the United States. But, they asserted, if the Corvette was built by a small factory in Italy, it would be considered one of the top automobiles in the world.

That said, *C/D*'s pundits went on to point out the essential philosophic inconsistency of the Corvette. "Duntov's primary aim in his professional life is to make the Corvette the finest sports car in the world. The styling department views his car as a unique opportunity to fool around with the swoopy shapes and flashing lights that somehow to them mean 'sport.'" Even so, Detroit's cubic-inch race had led Duntov to some inconsistencies of his

own. "It is known that Zora Arkus-Duntov is a great exponent of small-displacement, high-revving engines," the article continued. "[But] because he rightfully believes that his Corvette should represent the pinnacle of Chevrolet engineering, he cannot bring himself to accept producing his car with anything less than the biggest, most powerful engine in the Chevrolet line-up." That is, Duntov would never be content with a 5.7-liter Corvette when Chevy customers could order a 6.5-liter Malibu, and therefore the machine becomes bigger every year.

This couldn't go on, *C/D* concluded. New Chevrolet general manager John Z. DeLorean, an engineer himself, wouldn't stand for it. DeLorean wanted a 2600-pound Corvette powered by a 400-cubic-inch engine mounted behind the driver. "It remains uncertain if the new rear-engine version will be introduced in 1971 or 1972," *C/D* predicted.

In the meantime, however, there had to be one more conventional, front-engine Corvette. Its introduction was delayed until February—along with that of the all-new Camaro and Firebird—so that the first reports on it didn't appear until March 1970. The egg-crate grille returned, and similarly textured air outlets replaced the shark gills on the car's flanks (suggesting a similar feature on the "Tour de France" Ferraris of the late fifties). The fenders flared out a bit more, less for muscular effect than to protect the body sides from gravel thrown by the wide wheels. Reshaped seats added an inch of headroom.

Along with the slight face-lift, the hot-horsepower 350 finally arrived, with solid lifters, 11.0:1 compression, its very own pinstripe package, and the option designation LT1. The L88 option was gone—a casualty not only of federal emissions laws, but also of California noise regulations. Likewise, the triple-carb big blocks had proven too complicated to set up for the now requisite smog

gear. Chevrolet lengthened the old 427's $3^{49}/_{64}$-inch stroke to a full four inches for 454 cubic inches of displacement, but with emissions gear this new LS5 engine needed the extra cubes to make the same 390 bhp as its 427/4bbl predecessor. An aluminum-head LS7 version with 12.25:1 compression and 465 bhp was shown to the press but never actually produced. Fortunately, Chevy finally dropped the three-speed stick, making four-on-the-floor and Positraction standard.

So when *Road & Track* tested the most powerful '70 Corvette available in September 1970, it was a 390-bhp 454 with a single four-barrel carburetor. The bigger engine did deliver a bit more torque, and *R&T* called it

''by far the most tractable big-engine Corvette unit we've tried.'' A 3.08 final and Turbo Hydra-Matic transmission hampered acceleration times (15 seconds flat in the quarter, at 93 mph) but permitted a genuine top speed of 144 mph. Still, at 3740 pounds, the Corvette was rapidly growing too heavy for its aging chassis. *R&T*'s testers noted alarming brake fade and criticized the car for limited suspension travel that led to ''incompetence on all but the smoothest roads.''

It hardly mattered; Chevrolet had already shown the Corvette's mid-engine successor at the New York Auto Show in April. This stunning beauty maintained its Corvette identity with fender shapes from the current car—suitably toned down—and a boattail rear window just like that of the earlier Sting Ray. Called XP-882, the prototype carried its aluminum-head 454 V8 transversely, with a

chain-driven transmission tucked alongside the forward bank of cylinders. Up to that point, it resembled a Cadillac Eldorado/Olds Toronado driveline turned sideways. But in the XP-882, a bevel gear on the tranny's tail shaft drove a short propeller shaft—splined to allow for thermal expansion—*through* the engine's sump to a familiar Corvette differential and rear suspension. The entire setup had been designed to use as many existing Corvette and Eldorado/Toronado components as possible.

Structurally, the new car featured a steel monocoque frame, although it retained a fiberglass skin. And even with its big-block power plant, the prototype weighed only 2900 pounds. ''We have now established beyond a doubt that the car was indeed a prototype for future production—1973 to be exact,'' wrote *Road & Track* in January 1971. ''At this time, all major mechanical parts are 'locked in' and no more basic changes are likely to occur...."

Meanwhile, the existing Corvette soldiered on almost unchanged for 1971. A shift in corporate policy dictated lower compression ratios for all GM products that year—with a corresponding loss in horsepower. Nonetheless, *Car and Driver* tested four Corvettes in June, to compare the four different engines available.

C/D wrote that the basic L48 350, now rated 270 bhp, "specialized in painless performance"—faint praise for a power plant they found "quiet and completely without vice" and that still dragged a 3460-pound Corvette equipped with automatic transmission, air conditioning, and a 3.08:1 final drive through the quarter mile in 15.55 seconds at 90.36 mph. "Those who want to be comfortable and avoid the mechanical hassle but still go fast," the magazine continued, "should opt for the LS5, the 365-hp 454." That combination gave 14.20 seconds at 100.33 mph—again with automatic, air, and 3.08 gears—while sucking down Premium at the rate of 11 to 16 mpg.

"Corvette purists," the testers concluded, would prefer the LT1; even with its compression ratio trimmed from 11.25:1 down to 9.0:1, and with horsepower down to 330, "it hasn't lost the vibrant, high-strung personality that made it famous. It's eager and it talks to you." Backed up by a four-speed transmission and a 3.70 rear, the solid-lifter LT1 hustled through the quarter in 14.57 seconds at 100.55 mph. Naturally, the LS6 solid-lifter, aluminum-head 454 with a double-disc clutch and four-speed shifter turned the quickest time of all—13.8 seconds at 104.65 mph, even with a 3.36 rear. "It's Duntov's favorite engine," quipped the editors, but at $1220.70 only 200 buyers actually opted for it.

There were even fewer changes for 1972. Not surprisingly, the fast but expensive LS6 vanished from the

options list. *Motor Trend* decided to test every available Corvette, and wrote up the results in an article coyly titled "The Glass Menagerie." Acceleration times were similar to or slightly better than those clocked by *C/D* a year before, but *MT* also hired ace Corvette racer Tony DeLorenzo to herd the three 'Vettes around Riverside International Raceway. "It's probably the best-handling sports car I've driven on the street, bar none," said DeLorenzo of the LT1. "It think the only one that would come anywhere close to it would be the Ferrari Daytona." The basic L48 gave up almost nothing in handling to the LT1, but the heavy LS5 just couldn't match the small blocks' mannerly behavior, consistently running two to three seconds behind the LT1 in lap times.

In the same article, recreational vehicles editor Chuck Koch predicted a mid-engine Corvette by 1975. In Sep-

After a late (February) introduction and a short model run in 1970, the Corvette continued virtually unchanged in 1971—except that engine choices were down and emission requirements were already beginning to erode horsepower figures.

For 1972, Chevrolet dropped the Corvette's fiber-optic light monitor system and replaced it with a standard antitheft alarm. Externally, however, the '72 model closely resembled the '70–'71. The LT1 soldiered on for one last year, now down to 255 bhp but still the favorite of the automotive press. The year 1972 was the only time when Corvette buyers could order an LT1 with air-conditioning, and the example shown here is one of only 286 cars so equipped. Chevrolet engineers had feared that the high-winding LT1 engine would spin the air-conditioner belts right off their pulleys!

tember, *Road & Track* reported that GM had changed its mind regarding a mid-engine 'Vette for '73. Rising insurance premiums had taken a toll in Corvette sales—production dropped by more than 55 percent between 1969 (38,762) and 1970 (17,316), and the corporation believed that tightening emissions rules would only cut deeper into sporty-car sales. The '73 Corvette would be much like the '70-'72 model, modified to meet new bumper regulations. Beyond that, wrote *R&T*, ''a guess is as good as we can do. A major redesign of some kind does seem inevitable, though....'' The editors thought that, should the performance market shrink further, Chevrolet might build a steel-bodied Corvette sharing major chassis components with the Camaro.

In December 1972, Duntov revealed to *Car and Driver* the real reason the mid-engine car had been delayed: the engineers were just too damned busy modifying existing cars to meet safety and emissions rules.

C/D had already published photos of the real '73 'Vette in its July '72 issue. The front bumper could have been worse—a lot worse. The stylists managed to conceal the requisite steel battering ram inside a body-colored, molded-urethane housing that blended nicely with the Corvette's contours, even if it did increase front overhang by 2.2 inches. Inside, a tubular steel cross-member supported the bumper and doubled as a vacuum reserve tank for the headlight mechanism. This in turn removed one more bit of clutter from under the hood, which itself had been reshaped to accommodate either small or big-block engines and incorporated a cold-air intake flap at the rear. Just like the cowl induction systems already used on hot Chevelles and Camaros, it was opened by a solenoid whenever the throttle pedal hit the floor.

Fortunately, the new hood design also eliminated the complex and slow-moving concealed wiper mechanism.

tion—a change that, according to *C/D*, "completely transforms the Corvette's personality. It now has the smoothness and silence expected—but frequently not present—in a Grand Touring car."

Radial tires on theoretically optional aluminum wheels improved handling, eliminating much of the darting and nibbling of the wide, bias-belted tires used previously. Advertised horsepower plummeted—to 190 for the L48, and 275 for the big block (now with a revised camshaft and the designation LS4 on the options sheet). The LT1 gave way to the L82, a second hydraulic-lifter small block with "high" compression of 9.0:1 and 250 bhp at 5200 rpm. But as with the bumpers, this situation was not as bad as it seemed. Chevrolet, along with the rest of the industry, had switched from SAE (Society of Automotive Engineers) gross brake horsepower ratings to SAE net bhp; by the same standard, the previous year's L48 would have rated only 200 bhp, the LS5 would have rated 270, and the LT1 would have rated 255.

Motor Trend senior editor Eric Dahlquist liked the new LS4 better anyway, noting that the revised cam and cold air induction gave the big engine a livelier feel. His test car actually recorded better 0-speed times than the old LS5, up to 75 mph, and equalled its 14.1-second quarter-mile time.

C/D's testers missed the mechanical clatter of the solid-lifter LT1 but allowed that the new L82 wasn't a bad substitute. It still provided good performance with less weight—and therefore better handling with less effort—than the big block and still finished the quarter mile in 15.1 seconds at 95.4 mph (versus 14.6 at 95.7 for the LS4). "No other production sports car is so smooth and manageable at its limits," they wrote, "and none will cover for the driver's mistakes as quickly and easily as the Corvette." The year 1973 was a boom one for the auto industry, and the 'Vette rode the wave back up to 30,464 total sales.

U.S. federal bumper standards inspired the Corvette's 1973 face lift, although **Car and Driver,** *at least, found the new body-colored bumper an aesthetic improvement. Cleaner side vents matched the cleaner look up front, and a new engine hood incorporating standard cowl induction accommodated both small- and big-block motors.*

A simple reversed scoop (still functional) in the front fender replaced the Ferrari-like grate that had appeared there for the three previous years. "Overall," wrote *C/D*, "the '73 Corvette looks cleaner and more purposeful thanks to its front-end re-styling, but is still a disappointment to those who expected an all-new body or, better yet, an all-new mid-engine design for this year."

At the same time, Chevrolet eliminated the removable rear window on the coupe. Duntov told *Car and Driver* that this was to eliminate a "buffeting backdraft" that occurred with the roof off, the rear window out, and the side windows up—at 140 mph. Sure. The fixed window saved some weight, so that even with the heavy bumper and the steel guard beams in the doors, '73 Corvettes weighed only about 100 pounds more than their '72 equivalents.

And despite all the new federal requirements, Duntov's team had found time to engineer new rubber body mounts and to add a significant amount of sound insula-

"Word is just out, by the way," wrote *Motor Trend* in October 1972, "that the 'Vette will get a steel body in '75." Chevrolet would need the steel body to pass the 50-mph barrier crash test expected for 1976, said *MT*, and anyway, St. Louis now assembled enough Corvettes to make tooling up in steel profitable. "Contracts for bits and pieces have been awarded," the magazine reported. The editors speculated that the new car would be offered with the customer's choice of either reciprocating-piston or Wankel power.

Meanwhile, 1974 brought more of the same. The feds wanted a 5-mph bumper in the rear, too, so the 'Vette acquired a urethane tail to match its nose, and another 0.8 inch in length. Little else changed. *Car and Driver* wrote that the mid-engine 'Vette "has been delayed once again for at least another year"; *Motor Trend* now predicted that it would appear in 1977. But more demanding regulations were catching up with the Corvette. The 1975 models looked similar, but the front bumpers were now reinforced with plastic honeycomb and the rears were hydraulic, adding 140 pounds where it was needed least. The big-block engine failed its 50,000-mile emissions certification test and so had to be abandoned. Now equipped with a catalytic converter and single exhaust, the basic small block produced only 165 net bhp—the lowest number ever for a V8 Corvette —and the L82 produced only 205. Sales of the roadster had declined since 1969, and 1975 was acknowledged as the last year for the convertible Corvette.

On January 1, 1975, Zora Arkus-Duntov retired. And the new mid-engine Corvette remained, tantalizing as ever, just over the horizon.

In 1973 only, Corvettes carried a body-colored bumper up front and chrome bumperettes at the rear. The new bumper added 2.2 inches in front of the front wheels and, along with other changes, 100 pounds to the weight of the car. Radial tires were new that year as well.

CHAPTER FIVE

A COMFORTABLE SENESCENCE, 1976-82

The Corvette isn't just America's only sports car. It's America's last zoomy car.
Motor Trend, January 1973

Dave McLellan grew up in Detroit, with Detroit iron for transportation. He earned his mechanical engineering degree from Wayne State University, and landed a job solving noise, vibration, and harshness problems at GM's Milford Proving Grounds.

Then he bought his first foreign sports car—a 1957 Porsche 356B. It must have pleased him, because over the next decade he traded up for a 356C, then a 911, and became president of the Detroit-area Porsche Club. He also earned his master's degree in engineering and a spot on the team that designed the chassis for the 1970 Camaro. Then General Motors sent him to MIT as a Sloan fellow; he returned with his MBA in 1973, and in 1974 became Zora Arkus-Duntov's assistant. Still shaggy-haired and boyish at thirty-six years of age, McLellan succeeded Duntov as the Corvette's chief engineer in January 1975.

Duntov had left plans for a mid-engine Corvette with possible V8, V6, or even Wankel rotary power. McLellan knew he would have to choose one path for America's only sports car, and choose it soon. In the meantime, however, as he told *Car and Driver* contributing editor John Hilton in March 1983, he had "to keep the car healthy in the short term."

It wasn't going to be easy. An anonymous Chevrolet engineer admitted to *C/D* senior editor Brock Yates that "the Corvette is three feet too long and 800 pounds too heavy. Nobody in the Corporation has taken it seriously for five years simply because we've been able to sell all we could build without trying...."

Duntov had already completed the 1976 model. He went touring out west in a customized version with louvered roof pillars and a bubble-back rear window, leading *C/D* to wonder out loud if he had scheduled similar changes for the production version. He hadn't. The '76 Corvette looked almost exactly like the '75. The bumpers were stronger still, and to aim them more accurately the Corvette now rode a half-inch higher. A steel floor pan, welded to the existing roll cage, added rigidity and deflected heat from engines tuned to run hotter for higher efficiency. Cowl induction was abandoned in the name of sound reduction, replaced by a snorkel that sucked in air from over the radiator. But the L48 now produced 180 bhp at 4000 rpm, and the heavy-duty L82 made 210 at 5200. The heavy-duty Gymkhana suspension (first seen in 1974) remained on the options sheet, and the aluminum wheels announced back in 1973 became available at last.

Road & Track clocked an L82 with a 3.55 axle from 0 to 60 in 8.1 seconds and through the quarter mile in 16.5. "That's still pretty impressive performance these days," the editors concluded. *Car and Driver* recorded considerably better times with a 3.70 rear: 0 to 60 in 6.8, the quarter mile in 15.3. And Chevrolet sold 46,558 1976 Corvettes—a new record high.

McLellan scheduled a few more refinements for 1977, lengthening the gear shift lever by one inch and shortening the steering column by two, to better accommodate real-world human anatomy. A multifunction stalk on the steering column simplified the accessory switchgear, and a redesigned console accepted a wide variety of corporate (as opposed to Corvette-specific) sound systems. Glass roof panels appeared on some press cars, although supplier problems would keep them from the public for another year.

Also in 1977, the STINGRAY script vanished from the front fenders, replaced by a variation on the familiar Corvette crossed-flags emblem. The change was strangely symbolic, for Bill Mitchell left General Motors that year, to establish his own industrial design firm. Although he deliberately refrained from designing cars professionally, Bill continued to sketch and paint images of automobiles until he died in September 1988.

Motor Trend feature editor Tony Swan praised the '77 Corvette for the usual virtues (good brakes, unparalleled handling on a dry smooth road) and gently censured it for the usual vices (harsh ride, poor handling on wet roads, no room for human knees). *MT* clocked an automatic L82 with a 3.55 final from 0 to 60 in 8.8 seconds, and through the quarter mile in 16.6. "We're concentrating hard," McLellan told Swan, "on just trying to keep our performance where it was in 1975 through all the tightening emissions regulations that are coming."

But something even more interesting was going on. The base price of a new Corvette had risen steadily between 1955 and 1973, but now it was exploding by 10-

percent leaps, from $5562 in 1973 to $6002 in 1974, $6810 in 1975, $7605 in 1976, and now $8648 in 1977. At the same time, sales of this now clearly overweight, overwrought, and outmoded automobile *increased* almost as fast as the price, breaking the record again with 49,213 sold in 1977.

Car and Driver executive editor Patrick Bedard offered as good an explanation as anyone: "Even though the Corvette is a barefaced composite of old ideas," he wrote in March 1977, "it has little competition in the American marketplace." Or, as McLellan himself had told Swan a few months before, "It's still the fastest car made in America."

Still the speculation continued. GM's front-drive, "X-body" program was no longer a secret, and *Motor Trend* suggested that a mid-engine Corvette could be built around the driveline of the upcoming V6 Nova— the car that became the Chevrolet Citation.

Meanwhile, the '78 Corvette bowed with the bubble-back rear window—but without the louvered roof pillars —of Duntov's vacation vehicle. *Road & Track* feature edi-

On the outside, the '77 Corvette looked very similar to the '75–'76 model. But a new console, steering column, and shift lever significantly improved interior comfort. Almost symbolically, the Stingray name vanished from the Corvette the same year that Bill Mitchell left General Motors. This example features the optional aluminum wheels that were first shown to the press in 1973 but didn't reach production until 1976.

tor John Lamm thought that its compound-curved glass recalled the boattail Sting Ray from some angles. So did *Motor Trend*'s C. Paul Rogers. Certainly the glassy tail blended nicely with the glass roof panels, giving the impression that the whole top of the car was transparent, except for a body-colored band behind the seats.

Complementing the new look outside was a new instrument panel inside, with clean, rectilinear lines and, for the first time since 1967, a locking glove box. Mysteriously, the windshield-wiper switch migrated back to the dashboard—"a retrograde step," said *Motor Trend*. At the same time, Chevrolet announced a Silver Anniversary edition Corvette, painted two-tone silver (of course) and fitted with black, red, or "oyster" leather inside.

McLellan wanted a hatchback, but the fuel tank stood in the way, and moving it would have required a complete (and prohibitively expensive) redesign of the entire car from the seats on back. He did wangle enough funds

to enlarge the tank from seventeen to twenty-four gallons, a change that still required modifications to the frame, suspension, and exhaust system and demanded a space-saver spare. At the same time, he stiffened the standard suspensions of all but the automatic L48, slightly softened the rear shocks in the optional Gymkhana package, and added optional 255/60R-15 Goodyear GT radials. A new dual-snorkel air cleaner, combined with a less restrictive exhaust system, boosted the brake horsepower of the L82 to 220.

Car and Driver senior editor Brock Yates likened the Corvette to Jackie Onassis: "a subject of perpetual intrigue and fascination for the *vox populi* regardless of its age or impact on the larger scheme of things." That said, Yates allowed that the '78 'Vette was much improved: "Not only will it run faster now...but general driveability and road manners are of a high order as well....[with] handling that is certainly superior to any

Chevrolet celebrated the Corvette's twenty-fifth year by offering this special two-tone silver paint scheme. A bubble-back rear window not only improved visibility but expanded luggage space as well.

The new bubble-back rear for 1978 concealed a revised rear frame and significantly larger fuel tank. All '78 Corvettes—not just Silver Anniversary models like this one—sported 25th Anniversary emblems on the nose and fuel filler.

Going Like a Granatelli

Probably tens of thousands of Corvettes have been customized by their owners. But when Vince Granatelli stuffed an 880-bhp gas turbine into one in late 1979, *Motor Trend*, at least, took notice. The Pratt & Whitney ST6B turbine was one of four engines that Granatelli had left from his father's 1968 assault on Indianapolis. A wealthy customer had asked Granatelli for a street-legal turbine car, and Vince chose a Corvette for the job—partly for its handling, but mostly because its long nose provided enough room for a powerplant originally designed for stationary duty in an oil field. *MT* clocked 0 to 60 in 3.6 seconds and a quarter mile in 12 flat; Granatelli said the turbine Corvette would top 180 mph, and no one tried to prove him wrong.

[Corvette] in recent memory.'' *C/D*'s automatic L48 with a 3.08 rear and standard 70-profile tires reached 60 mph from rest in just 7.8 seconds, charged through the quarter in 16.1, and topped out at 123 mph.

Yates pointed out that the new rear window expanded the Corvette's usable luggage capacity—even if you did still have to load it through the roof and doors. And he sagely noted the real significance of the much-revised glass-back Corvette: the investment it represented meant that GM expected to sell the same basic car until at least 1981. Although ably assisted by Jim ''Jingles'' Ingle, Art Beaumont, Gib Hufstader, and maybe half a dozen other engineers, McLellan simply didn't have the staff to produce an all-new car anytime in the foreseeable future. Still, the chief engineer himself told Yates that he wanted to pare 200 pounds from the Corvette by 1980.

Meanwhile, a Corvette was chosen to pace the 1978 Indianapolis 500, an honor which launched yet another two-tone special edition. While anniversary 'Vette's wore their lighter hue on top, Pace Car replicas reversed the scheme, with a black upper body separated from a silver lower body by a red pinstripe. Red stripes also ringed the aluminum wheels. Front and rear spoilers and special seats completed the package. Chevrolet numbered the Pace Cars (but not the anniversary editions) separately and sold 6,502 of them. Total sales for 1978 fell slightly, to 46,776.

Nearly the same seats appeared on all Corvettes in 1979, and the spoilers became a $265 option—although fewer than 13 percent of all Corvette buyers ordered them. (GM told *Road & Track* that the air dams reduced aerodynamic lift by 53 percent in front and 97 percent in the rear—at 130 mph.) McLellan applied the L82's low-restriction intake and exhaust system to the L48, raising its output to 195 bhp, while an auxiliary electric radiator fan left 5 more bhp available for the L82 itself. *Car and Driver*

timed one of the latter (with four-speed transmission and a 3.70 rear) from 0 to 60 in 6.6 seconds and through the quarter-mile in 15.3, and noted a top speed of 127 mph. But *C/D* technical editor Don Sherman excoriated the Corvette for its poor directional stability and its "loose and lazy" feel. The new seats felt worse than the ones they'd replaced (which were pretty bad), and the optional 60-series tires only exacerbated the 'Vette's poor directional stability and twitchy tail end. "The time has come to pass the crossed flags on to the next generation," he concluded. Yet, while marveling at "the hordes outbidding each other for an obsolete sports car," Sherman did mention that the 'Vette was still "capable of turning in the best performance profile of any American car."

In 1979, the outbidding horde numbered 53,807, another new record.

McLellan had shared some of his future plans with Sherman late in 1978. To save weight in the 1980 Corvette, McLellan would replace the powdered talc used as filler in the body panels with tiny air bubbles. He also planned to redesign the frame, replace the 'Vette's fourteen-year-old brakes with the lighter discs recently developed for the downsized E-body cars (Eldorado/Toronado/Riviera), and use aluminum casings for the transmission and differential. A carbon-fiber leaf spring would save more weight in the rear, and plastic wheels loomed as a real possibility. But McLellan refused to surrender V8 power; he said he'd downsize to Chevy's 305 cubic-inch V8 if he had to, but would go no smaller than that.

The chief engineer also revealed his plans for an all-new Corvette for the 1983 model year. He had tried the mid-engine, Nova-based route, installing the soon-to-be-Citation suspension and driveline in a Porsche 914. He didn't like the result. McLellan's Corvette would still carry its engine in front, tied through a torque tube to a rear-mounted transaxle. It sounded like Duntov's Q-Corvette, resurrected after thirty years, but in fact Porschephile McLellan had locked his sights on a different

Introduced after the Silver Anniversary car, the Pace Car replica reversed the former's two-tone paint scheme, resulting in a dark upper and light lower body. Technical improvements for all '78 'Vettes included revised suspension tuning, more powerful engines, and a larger fuel tank. But after steady growth since 1970, Corvette sales hiccuped in 1978, dipping to 46,776.

target: the Porsche 924. He would also dispense with the Corvette's separate ladder frame entirely and use subframes to tie all mechanical components to the cage around the passenger compartment. In true Duntovian style, he believed he could lift the front suspension from the contemporary Malibu and modify the existing Corvette rear suspension, controlling deflection steer with new transverse links behind the halfshafts.

The styling, said McLellan, would simply have to be reeled in a bit. "Batwing fenders will be planed smooth," wrote Sherman. "The wasp-waisted passenger bay will be filled out for more elbowroom, and a couple of feet will be chopped from the overall length." Sherman himself predicted a wheelbase of 96 inches, a weight of 2700 pounds, an engine output of 180 bhp, and a quarter mile in 16 seconds. GM still hadn't approved the project when Sherman interviewed McLellan for the December 1978 issue. The following September, however, *C/D* reported that the new Corvette program was under way and due to deliver in the 1984 model year.

Meanwhile, McLellan met his weight goal for 1980 and then some. Most noticeable were the newly shaped bumpers at both ends, which nicely integrated the spoilers that had been optional the year before. What couldn't be seen was that the bumpers now were made from fiberglass instead of steel. McLellan delivered the lighter frame he promised, along with an aluminum case for the differential (but not for the transmission). The window glass was thinner, and glass beads were introduced as a weight-reducing filler in the roof panels. As a result, the 1980 Corvette weighed in 238 to 321 pounds lighter than the '79, depending on whose numbers you believe.

On the down side, the General had saved itself some money by certifying fewer drivelines with the U.S. Environmental Protection Agency. The L82 now produced 230 bhp, but came only with an automatic transmission. Most

U.S. buyers could still order an L48 with a four-speed, but the only engine available to Californians was the LG4: a 180-bhp 305 with automatic transmission and—to save more weight—stainless steel exhaust manifolds.

The weight reduction produced surprisingly little effect on acceleration (*Car and Driver* measured 0 to 60 in 7.6 seconds and a quarter mile in 15.9 for a four-speed L48 with a 3.07 rear), but it seemed to improve handling. Of course, the switch from the optional 225/60R-15 aramid-belted tires to steel-belted Goodyear Eagle GTs of the same size probably helped as well. "Steering response is accurate and predictable now," wrote Bedard, now *C/D*'s editor-at-large, "vastly better than in the test cars we drove just a few years ago." Still, Bedard reported that the Corvette "creaks, groans, and protests" when driven over even slightly rough surfaces. The once-limber shifter had grown stiff in comparison to more modern

After a mild face-lift in 1980, Corvette styling continued unchanged in 1981. However, the '81 Corvette pioneered GM's glass-reinforced plastic "Monoleaf" rear spring—at least on automatic transmission editions with the standard suspension. And electronic control of the fuel mixture and ignition timing— exclusive to California in 1980—spread to all fifty states in 1981.

units. And he also lamented the lack of decor in the engine bay: ''Gone is the chrome. Gone are the cast-aluminum rocker covers. Except for the radio shielding over the spark-plug wires, which is now done in black plastic instead of bright metal, you could just as well be looking at the powerplant of an El Camino.''

Still, new *C/D* executive editor Mike Knepper seemed to grasp the Corvette's essential paradox. ''Despite the deserved vilification the car gets around the office,'' he wrote, ''it's the first to disappear from the parking lot....I drive it and I'm infuriated by all the things wrong with it, and thoroughly entertained.''

The year 1981 brought more weight-saving measures, most notably a *fiberglass* rear leaf spring for automatic models. It weighed only eight pounds, against the forty-four-pound stack of steel leaves it replaced. For the first time since 1954, there were no engine options—just a 190-

bhp 350 called L81. At least it could be ordered all over with a four-speed. With electronic fuel and ignition controls and stainless-steel exhaust manifolds adapted from the LG4, it developed the same peak horsepower as the late L48 but at a slightly milder 4200 rpm.

More significantly, 1981 was the year that Chevrolet opened a new factory for Corvette production. The so-called mill building in St. Louis was built in the twenties to produce the structural wooden pieces then used in GM car bodies. By the late seventies, the number of Corvettes that could be built there each year was limited as much by lack of floor space as it was by the age of the equipment. The first Corvette rolled off the new line in Bowling Green, Kentucky, on June 1, although parallel production continued in St. Louis through August 1.

To enthusiasts everywhere, the new factory meant a new Corvette was finally on its way. Suddenly, after all the

Right: Chevrolet built 1981 Corvettes in both St. Louis, Missouri, and Bowling Green, Kentucky. The cars from both plants are identical except for their paintwork; St. Louis used lacquer, while Bowling Green favored enamel base coats with a clear coat on top. Apparently this led to the popular, but untrue impression that St. Louis produced only solid-color cars while Bowling Green built the two-tones. Below right: Fuel injection returned to the Corvette for 1982 in the form of a simplified dual throttle-body system that Chevrolet called "cross fire" injection. Opposite page, top: Chevrolet reintroduced two-tone paint for the Corvette in 1981. A modest 4,871 buyers opted for a two-color Corvette in 1982, the year this coupe was produced. Opposite page, bottom: More buyers than that—6,759—chose the 1982 Collector Edition, painted a handsome silver-beige with fadeaway stripes.

dead-end prototypes and broken promises, the advent of an all-new car seemed not only real but certain.

A new engine appeared the very next year. Actually, it was still the familiar small-block 350, but with 9.0:1 compression, cast-aluminum pistons, and a re-profiled cam. Up top sat an aluminum cross-ram manifold with a pair of single-barrel throttle bodies, each packing its own fuel-injection nozzle. Chevrolet called this latter system "cross-fire injection," which, quipped *Road & Track*, "sounded more like a malfunction than a sales feature."

Nonetheless, the fuelie 'Vette had returned, after a sixteen-year hiatus—even if it lacked the deep-breathing plenum and individual port nozzles of the 1957 system. Producing 200 bhp at 4400 rpm and 285 pound-feet of torque at 2800 rpm, this "L83" engine found its way into every 1982 Corvette built. Backing it up was just one transmission, a four-speed automatic with a 0.70:1 overdrive top. The new gearbox featured a 3.06:1 first gear, which was considerably shorter than the 2.52:1 first found previously in automatic 'Vettes, and required stronger U-joints to cope with the additional torque multiplication.

Outside, the '82 Corvette had changed very little, but Chevrolet did offer a special Collector Edition package with silver-beige paint, gold trim, and gray tape stripes that faded away from darker to lighter tones. Cast aluminum wheels consciously copied the 1967 design, and the rear window lifted up on a pair of gas struts—a half-way hatchback that required no major revisions to body or chassis. Collector Editions were numbered separately from other Corvettes, and 6,759 of them left Bowling Green on their way to happy buyers.

Road & Track liked the throttle response of the new engine, and timed an '82 Corvette from 0 to 60 mph in 7.9 seconds, while making the quarter-mile run in 16.1 seconds at 84.5 mph. "At last a relief from years of backsliding," sighed the editors, although the stiff chassis and massive body, neither changed in any significant way, still felt "sort of like a go kart under a homecoming float." In 1982, sports cars no longer needed to ride that badly to handle that well.

Furthermore, the Corvette's base price had now more than doubled in five years, to $18,290. (Chevrolet wanted $22,538 for Collector Editions.) Sales had fallen steadily since 1979's peak, and with a new Corvette now a certainty, they plummeted in 1982 to 25,407.

Despite the car's many shortcomings, *Road & Track* shed an editorial tear for the passing of the Stingray. "The basic honesty of the car rises above its own image," wrote the road testers. "The car has its own particular flavor and appeal, and the automotive world would lose a great deal if the Corvette were to become too much like other automobiles."

They needn't have worried about that.

CHAPTER SIX

CORVETTE, THE NEXT GENERATION, 1984-88

My model of the Corvette is that everything it does it better do better than anybody else—it's the King of the Hill game.

David R. McLellan

From *Car and Driver,* March 1983

Page 94: *After more than a decade of dead-ends, delays, and speculation, an all-new Corvette finally arrived in March 1983—promoted by Chevrolet as an "early '84" model. The engine remained in front of the driver, but the new 'Vette did employ some fairly exotic technology in the design of its body, frame, and suspension.* Page 95: *"You could see the convertible in the car," Studio Chief Jerry Palmer told* **Automobile Quarterly** *in 1986. GM stylists had sketched convertible versions of the new-generation Corvette as early as 1979. Virtually everyone recognized that the new coupe was a higher business priority, however, so serious development of a convertible didn't even begin until early 1984. When the new roadster finally appeared in 1986, a bright yellow example was chosen to pace the Indianapolis 500.* Opposite page: *The first of a new generation poses with its most distant ancestor.*

Born in Detroit in 1942, Jerry Palmer studied transportation design at the Detroit Art School for the Society of Arts and Crafts. Among his teachers there was Alex Tremulis, the self-taught aerodynamic genius behind the Tucker. A summer internship at GM Design led to full-time employment in 1966. There, Palmer worked on projects ranging from the spectacular, Sting Ray-esque '71 boat-tail Riviera to the ill-fated but graphically interesting Cosworth Vega before leaving for a three-month stint at Isuzu in Japan. He returned to Detroit and the incubating Chevrolet Monza in 1972. With Henry Haga and Chuck Jordan (later GM Design vice president), he helped Bill Mitchell develop the mid-engine Aerovette show car. In 1974, Palmer succeeded Haga as the studio chief of Chevrolet Exterior 3. The '82 Camaro and Firebird that he created there not only won critical acclaim but also established his style as an automobile designer.

A die-hard race fan, Palmer particularly admired the form of Pininfarina's Ferrari 308. He finally bought himself one in the early eighties. Before that, however, Palmer had owned and driven Corvettes—no less than seven between 1968 and 1980.

Palmer borrowed elements from Mitchell's Aerovette to create a more restrained and modern mid-engine Corvette proposal in the spring of 1975. The car would have been quite handsome, but it died a quiet death when McLellan parked his Citation-powered 914 for the last time in late 1977. The next Corvette would follow a very different theme.

Fairly accurate photos of the car that would be the all-new Corvette appeared in the enthusiast magazines in January 1982. Palmer had carefully preserved the shape, proportion, and even many details of the '68-'82 cars, while filling out the passenger space and flattening the fender flares down to a more symbolic level. Perhaps he had shunned an all-new design to pay tribute to the past, but the 1968-generation Corvette had been the *only* Corvette for so long, how could he have done anything else? The new car elicited not so much a "Wow!" as an "Of course!" This was the Corvette that Zora Arkus-Duntov probably wanted the '68 to be.

The first tests appeared about a year later, in March 1983, when the new Corvette went on sale as a 1984 model. GM's market mavens wouldn't say why they had simply skipped a model year, but *Road & Track* thought that the corporation may have been better able to absorb the thirsty Corvette into its federally mandated Corporate Average Fuel Economy (CAFE) in the 1984 model year. The 1982 Corvettes were still sold and registered as such through February 1983. The General registered some prototypes of the new car as '83s, but those sold to the public were all '84s.

"Whatever your views of previous Corvettes," wrote *Road & Track* in March 1983, "forget them."

Although he could not have revealed it at the time, McLellan had already chosen the basic layout of the new Corvette in 1978. He had also developed a "mission statement" for the car, which he later outlined in *Corvette: The Legend Lives On*: "If something that is a uniquely Corvette characteristic is worth doing, then it is worth doing better than anybody else....If the car is supposed to go fast, for example, it might as well go faster than anything else....I'd be the first one to admit that at times we've even compromised the ride quality of the Corvette as a passenger car to achieve a handling objective."

A mid-engine layout, he told *Car and Driver* editor-at-large Brock Yates in March 1983, took up too much passenger space, and a V6, well, ''It was simply not a Corvette.'' And that, McLellan had decided, was the most important criterion of all: that a new Corvette should remain acceptable to people who already owned and loved the older models. As he wrote in *The Legend Lives On*, ''They have so much of themselves tied up in it that in a way we're merely the custodians of the Corvette. Their attitude is to say, 'Well, what are you doing to *my* car next year?' That's a sobering way to look at it.'' The fact that GM had already approved development of the '82 front-engine, V8-powered Camaro and Firebird in 1976 no doubt influenced his decision as well.

Actually, the 1984 Corvette had strayed very little from the concept that McLellan had outlined for *Car and Driver*'s Don Sherman in December 1978. The gearbox had moved up to a more conventional position behind the engine, and instead of a torque tube, an aluminum channel on the right side of the drive shaft connected the casing of the transmission to the casing of the differential. It looked less like a Porsche drivetrain than what McLellan had originally described, but the effect was the same: it acted as a single, rigid, self-supporting unit.

This self-supporting driveline allowed McLellan to dispense with any crossmembers under the passenger compartment, which in turn allowed a lower profile for the whole car while retaining acceptable ground clearance and head room. To bring the car down even lower, McLellan tucked the single-catalyst exhaust system directly *under* the propeller shaft, where its height was absorbed by the high driveline tunnel.

McLellan also delivered the sheet-steel "uniframe" he had promised, incorporating the cowl and windshield frame in front of the passengers, a rollover hoop behind them, and massively tall steel channels in the door sills. But he didn't have to borrow any suspension components from any parts bin. Although he retained a double-wishbone layout up front, the pieces were all new and unique to the Corvette, while the all-new body allowed the three-degree caster that the 'Vette needed so badly for directional stability. In the rear, fixed-length halfshafts still doubled as upper lateral links. But the old 'Vette's single trailing arm per side gave way to upper and lower trailing links, and—again as McLellan had promised in '78—a tie rod behind the spring controlled toe-in changes under cornering loads. The springs themselves, front and rear, were not carbon fiber but Liteflex fiberglass-reinforced epoxy; lab tests showed they would last sixty-seven times longer than springs made of steel.

McLellan didn't even buy the brakes from General Motors; GM's own Delco Moraine Division hadn't been able to meet his standards, so he ordered lightweight discs from Girlock, an Australian joint venture between Girling and AP-Lockheed that already supplied the down-under divisions of Ford, GM, Toyota, Nissan, and Mitsubishi—as well as most Formula 1 racing teams.

In fact, the only chassis piece borrowed from any other GM car was the Citation steering rack, and even this was heavily modified for a more linear response and better road feel. The standard steering ratio was 15.5:1; Corvettes equipped with the Z51 handling option featured an ultra-quick 13.0:1. The standard tires were again Goodyear Eagle GT's, size 215/65R-15, mounted on 15x7-inch aluminum wheels in front and 15x7.5-inch rims in the rear, while Z51s rode on 16x8.5 fronts and 16x9.5 rears shod with 255/50VR-16 Goodyear Eagle VR50s. Actually, no wheel on an '84 Corvette would exchange with any other, for not only were the rear wheels wider than the front wheels, but the brake cooling slots curved in different directions on the right and left sides.

Temporarily, at least, the new Corvette inherited the cross-fire injection engine from its immediate predecessor. Now called L98, minor revisions to the intake, exhaust, and accessory drives raised its net horsepower to 205 at 4300 rpm, and torque to 290 pound-feet at 2800. But a handsome, sculptured air cleaner housing and rocker covers of die-cast magnesium brought some visual excitement back to the Corvette engine bay. At the same time, Chevrolet promised that a port fuel-injection system—close in principle to the '57-'65 model—was in the pipeline. The four-speed automatic remained the only transmission option at first, but a Doug Nash four-speed joined it later in the model year, coupled to a planetary overdrive of 0.76:1. The overdrive existed primarily to satisfy the U.S. EPA and engaged automati-

Opposite page, top: The vertical thrust of a modern urban skyline is slashed by the powerfully horizontal '84 Corvette. Yet both forms epitomize the latest in functional engineering.

Opposite page, bottom: The 1984 Corvette's digital-electronic instruments—like the 1953's Powerglide transmission—seemed really cool at the time. But with crisp three-color graphics, automatic brightness regulation, and manual controls that allowed the driver to switch off some of the clutter, the Corvette's digital-electronic display was by far the best ever produced, anywhere in the world, for an automobile.

to incorporate the more rounded surface development of Mitchell's Aerovette—and of the existing production car. Palmer consciously decided to swap the old car's wasp waist for a lower profile, and McLellan's group accommodated him by moving the exhaust and steering gear out of the way. The characteristic Corvette shark gills were a fairly late addition, inspired by designer John Cafero's November 1979 rendering of an open-topped racer. Palmer quickly embraced the idea; as he told *Car and Driver* associate editor Jean Lindamood, "The car needed some *scars*." Its front fascia emerged last and related closely to that of the mid-engine prototype that Chevrolet had shown in New York in 1970, as well as to the revised front bumper of the '80-'82 production cars —except that where those cars had air intakes (which were essentially nonfunctional), the new Corvette sported light clusters.

GM's executive director of interior design George Moon demanded electronic instruments. Palmer resisted at first, then decided that a liquid-crystal gauge panel fit the Corvette's high-tech image. "They don't send up a Saturn rocket by looking at dials," he told *Automobile Quarterly* in the summer of 1986, and it seemed he was right. At first, Pat Furey's interior design group tried a number of floating-pod themes for the Corvette dash, but Design vice president Irvin Rybicki (who was Mitchell's successor) vetoed that idea as unworkable when GM management insisted on a passenger-side crash pad. This latter requirement, unique to the Corvette, more or less forced the relatively conservative shape of the '84 Corvette dashboard.

Car and Driver liked the new car, beginning with its looks. "The shape is clean and forthright," wrote Yates, "with none of the phallic silliness that distinguished its predecessor during its protracted career." Compared to that predecessor, the new Corvette measured nearly

Externally, only its unpainted wheel centers and roof-mounted brake light mark this Corvette as a 1986 model. Internally, however, the engineers had made significant improvements to the driveline, suspension, and brakes in 1985; then for 1986 they added antilock braking and an antitheft system that "read" the electrical resistance of a pellet imbedded in the ignition key.

cally in second, third, and fourth gears whenever an on-board computer judged road speed and throttle position to be appropriate for it.

Export Corvettes, incidentally, all left the factory on Z51 springs, shocks, and sway bars, but with the slower steering ratio and 16x8.5-inch wheels at both ends. They also featured a lockout switch for the automatic overdrive—something U.S. journalists would wish for earnestly.

The exterior styling theme had originated as a sketch by Palmer in 1978, and by October of that year had very nearly reached its definitive form in full-size clay. If anything, that model was judged to be a little *too* restrained —and perhaps a little too close to the Camaro that had just emerged from Studio Three—so over the next twelve months Palmer's staff very gradually refined the design

nine inches shorter and two inches wider, and rode on the two-inch shorter wheelbase that *C/D*'s Sherman had predicted in December 1978. But it was the new Corvette's performance that really impressed Yates: 0 to 60 in 6.7 seconds, a 15.2-second quarter mile at 90 mph, and a top speed over 140 mph. "These figures qualify the Corvette as one of the half-dozen fastest production automobiles in the entire world!" he exclaimed.

Moreover, the new Corvette could corner faster than any other street car on the planet, reaching a lateral acceleration of 0.90 g at a time when the best Ferraris and Porsches could manage only 0.82, and its 70 to 0 mph braking performance bettered that of the Porsche 928 and missed that of the Porsche 930—the best yet tested by *C/D*—by less than a car length.

Road & Track obtained similar results: 0.896 g on the skid pad, which was approached only by the 0.869 of the vaunted Lamborghini Countach. *R&T* added that only the Countach, along with the Ferrari 512 BB and the mid-engine Renault R5 Turbo II, could top the Corvette's slalom speed of 63.8 mph. Moreover, they found the plastic Chevy's handling "a delight"—even on less-than-perfect surfaces, where the Z51 "displayed none of the chiropractic chagrin of the older Corvette's slalom suspension." Vastly improved seats helped. The *R&T* staff couldn't agree on the 'Vette's electronic instruments and excused its "4 + 3" gearbox, pointing out that the latter provided an automatic kickdown for passing at highway speeds—and that a heavy right foot kept the overdrive at bay.

The long-awaited Corvette convertible returned in February 1986. Note how the lid that covers the top cuts down into the rear quarter panels; this was done to keep rainwater from pooling in the top's storage compartment.

In August, *R&T* European editor Paul Frère tried a Z51 Corvette at Goodyear's test track in Luxembourg. "Sensational," he exclaimed. "I feel certain this is the best handling road car on road tires I have ever driven." Frère wished only for more road feel from the steering—and wondered how the Z51's rock-hard suspension would fare outside the confines of a closed test course.

Despite all its re-engineering, however, the Corvette weighed more than it should have. "At 3300 pounds," quipped Yates, "[it] carries no advantage over the old flying dildo." Despite what *C/D* measured on its scales, in fact, Chevrolet claimed a curb weight of only 3117 pounds. By 1982, however, even the *old* Corvette had been pared down to within 230 pounds of that. Chevrolet hinted broadly at an aluminum-block engine to solve the problem.

Refinements arrived in 1985. Most significant was the promised port fuel injection, which boosted the output of the L98 engine to 230 bhp at 4000 rpm, took the torque up to 330 pound-feet—and at the same time stretched its fuel efficiency by 10 percent! Word passed quietly that the Corvette could now top 150 mph in stock trim. Apparently Chevrolet briefly considered "Life begins at 150" as an advertising slogan before its liability lawyers torpedoed the idea.

Responding to customer complaints, McLellan softened the front springs somewhat, by 26 percent in the base car and 16 percent in the Z51. Both cars benefited from 25 percent softer springs in the rear. To compensate, the Z51 now packed even stiffer antiroll bars, Bilstein gas-filled shock absorbers, and a heavy-duty cooling package.

Antilock brakes, adapted from the Bosch ABS system, followed for all Corvettes in 1986, along with three more degrees of caster in the front suspension for even better on-center steering feel. Aluminum heads were supposed to have relieved the engine bay of about forty pounds, but early examples cracked, and they were withdrawn from production—temporarily, at least.

In January of that year, Chevrolet made the announcement that the Corvette had been chosen to be the official Pace Car for the Indianapolis 500. Interestingly, the last car that had paced the race without engine modifications had been the 1978 Corvette. With its new-found performance, the new '86 Corvette would handle its Pace-Car duties in its showroom trim as well, leading Chevrolet general manager Bob Burger to comment, "Every Corvette we build in 1986 will be equipped with a genuine Pace-Car engine."

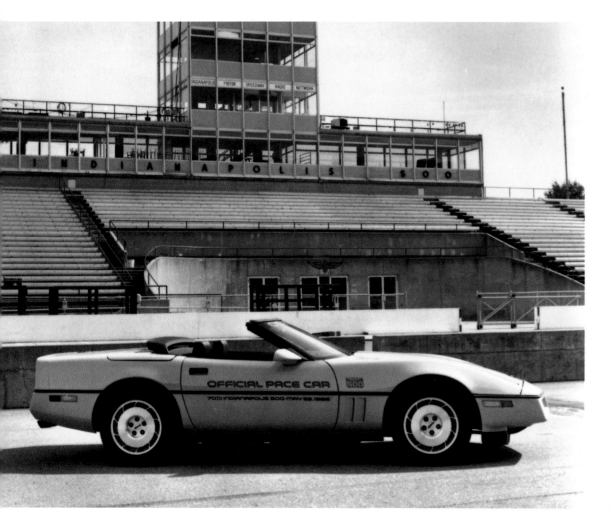

The actual 1986 Corvette Pace Car, photographed at the Indianapolis Motor Speedway. Note the subtle faring behind the seats; this housed the lights that were used to signal the race cars following behind.

More significant, the Corvette Pace Car would be a *convertible*, the first of a new series of production roadsters. After a ten year absence, the Corvette Convertible was back.

"We at Design Staff always wanted a convertible," Palmer told AQ in 1986. "It was always in the backs of our minds....you could see the convertible in the car." Indeed, you could: back in 1984, the John Cafero rendering that contributed the 'Vette's shark gills had shown the car shamelessly topless—and it wasn't the only rendering that did. "But because of the complexity of introducing the new car," Palmer continued, "it just wasn't in the cards for 83½."

GM engineers had begun discussing a convertible Corvette in early 1984 with the American Sunroof Corporation (ASC), which already built limited-production drop tops for American Motors as well as the General.

Then, in June of that year, ASC simply delivered a ragtop prototype to GM's doorstep.

It was evident that the prototype needed a lot of work. The fiberglass-over-steel structure of the Corvette coupe wasn't the stiffest in the world, and chopping off the top sure didn't help the problem any. McLellan's engineers raised the entire car 0.39 inch to provide room for an X-brace under the seats. An additional crossmember joined the rear wheel arches, substituting for the rollover hoop. Then they beefed up the crossmember under the engine, the K-braces connecting the frame rails to the crossmember, the front torque box, and the flat panel located behind the seats. Even the mounting for the steering gear and the door latches themselves were changed for convertible duty. Softer shocks and wide, 9.5-inch tires worked to minimize stress on the structure, and, needless to say, the Z51 option was simply not available.

The striking yellow of the Indianapolis Pace Car looked equally good on the '86 Corvette coupe. Chevrolet had not painted a production Corvette yellow since 1981.

Below: Subtle refinements improved the already outstanding legibility of the Corvette instrument panel in 1985. This identical example dates from 1986. Opposite page, top: This 1986 Malcom Konner Commemorative Edition Corvette is one of fifty coupes finished in a distinctive silver-beige-over-black paint scheme for America's largest Corvette dealer. Opposite page, bottom: The unpainted wheel center marks this as a 1986 model.

With all those modifications, *Road & Track* feature editor Steve Kimball thought the convertible rode better than the coupe. "Everything about the car feels smoother, better balanced, and more comfortable," he wrote. "The shakes are gone from the cowl, the steering wheel, and even the seat." Convertible production began in January 1986—with 9.5:1 aluminum heads exclusive to the roadster. Despite the increased compression, Chevrolet claimed no additional horsepower. But the lighter heads, combined with the elimination of the all-glass hatch, just about balanced the weight added by the structural bracing, so that the Corvette Convertible weighed little more than the coupe.

To commemorate the Corvette's Indianapolis adventure, Chevrolet designated *all* Corvette Convertibles sold that year as Pace Car replicas, and they all carried dash plaques to prove it. The appropriate decal package came in the luggage bin, where, as Palmer told AQ, "it is up to [the buyer] if he wants to stick them on or not—or keep them for posterity or put them on his kid's wagon."

And at the auto shows that year, Chevrolet presented the Corvette Indy, a mid-engine, four-wheel-drive prototype coupe. Among its interesting features was a drive-by-wire accelerator: the pedal on the floor communicated directly with the engine computer, which in turn decided how far to open the throttle plate.

McLellan shared his plans for the '87 model in mid-1986. "We're introducing a new suspension performance option which we're going to call Z52," he told *Automobile Quarterly.* "Basically, it's all the things that Z51 was; it has the secondary cooling fan, the engine oil cooler. It uses the 9½-inch wheels, the fast steering ratio and appropriate stabilizer bars, but the spring rates are the standard spring rates." All Z52s would feature their own Bilstein shocks, and Z52 coupes would use the entire, reinforced front structure of the convertible in order to compensate for the stiffer sway bars. "By having the Z52," McLellan continued, "we can package both the coupe and the convertible as a really super highway car." The Z51 would indeed continue—with the same structural improvements—but it would be restricted to manual-transmission coupes only.

When *Car and Driver* tested all three variations (base, Z51, and Z52) in June 1987, technical editor Csaba Csere found bigger differences in ride than in handling. And despite its stiffer shocks, the Z52 rode smoother than the base car on anything less than perfect pavement, "practically eliminating the base car's front-end quiver and chassis flex." The Z51, of course, felt "significantly harsher." The Z52 also topped its stablemates on the skid pad (0.87 g versus 0.86 for both base and Z51), where the base car was hampered by its narrower wheels ("only" 8.5 inches) and the Z51 by strong understeer. Understeer also limited the Z51's performance on an Autocross course, where it was beaten by both the Z52 *and* the base car. Only on Willow Springs Raceway

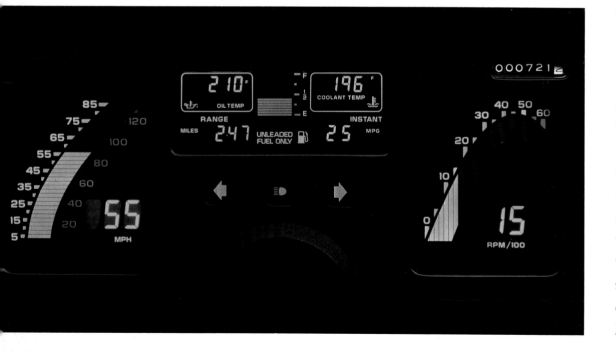

did the Z51 demonstrate an advantage; there, its front-heavy roll bias inspired driver confidence and kept the tail in check while powering through the turns. C/D's conclusion? Ideally, Csere said he'd take a Z52 but with the base steering ratio, which he found "easier to live with in real-world driving." Unfortunately, Chevrolet didn't offer that combination.

At the 1987 Geneva auto show, ASC debuted the Corvette Genève, featuring chromed, seventeen-inch wheels (already scheduled for '88 production) and rounder, more consciously sculptured surfaces. *Car and Driver* thought the body contours might forecast the 1990 Corvette. At the same time, *C/D* published pictures of an all-aluminum, 350 cubic-inch V8 with four overhead cams and thirty-two valves. The editors thought that this "LT5" engine, developed by Lotus, would appear in the '89 Corvette.

Road & Track reported in January that GM had again considered a mid-engine 'Vette, this time a space-frame model that could share production space with a redesigned Pontiac Fiero. "Certainly a mid-engine car will be one of the contenders," McLellan had told *AQ* the year before. "I don't think we would do another front-engine, rear-wheel-drive car at this point in time."

One bizarre bit of Corvette evolution that did reach the showroom floor was the Callaway Twin Turbo, rated 345 bhp and with 465 pound-feet of torque. Callaway Engineering in Old Lyme, Connecticut, performed the conversion, which buyers could order through Chevrolet dealers as RPO B2K. The Twin-Turbo Corvette could bolt to 60 mph in five seconds flat and reach 178 mph at the top end—yet Chevrolet warranted everything but the driveline, and Callaway warranted that. Only 184 buyers opted for the option in 1987.

In 1988, Chevrolet marked the Corvette's thirty-fifth anniversary with another special anniversary-edition car, this one nearly monochrome white below the belt line, topped with a black roof panel and rollover hoop. White painted wheels and a white leather interior complemented the special paint job, and the car arrived with many luxury features standard. Bowling Green built 2050 of them—a fraction of the 15,283 (admittedly more attractive) twenty-fifth anniversary editions sold a decade earlier.

The new seventeen-inch wheels for Z51 and Z52 that year came shod with 275/40ZR-17 Goodyear Eagles. All Corvettes had benefitted from the aluminum 9.5:1 heads since 1987, when Chevy also upped the horsepower rating of the L98 to 240. For 1988, a less restrictive exhaust system added another 5 bhp, but only for coupes with the 3.07:1 axle. Other improvements included further suspension revisions, and refinements to the brakes and air conditioning. *Car and Driver*'s May 1988 cover pronounced the '88 model the "Best Vette Yet," and inside Csere called it "one of the world's great supercar bargains."

At the same time, however, the technical editor admitted that "the arguments between staff members who are smitten with the Corvette's speed and those who are discouraged by its deficiencies never stop." Csere praised the Z52 test car for "handling more benignly than any other Corvette we've ever driven.... You can play Mario Andretti all day long without fearing that the chassis will snap into oversteer the first time you make a little mistake." Even with an automatic transmission, the Corvette reached 60 mph in 5.6 seconds, blasted through the quarter mile in 14.3 at 95 mph, and topped out at an impressive 154. Still, the squeaks and rattles inherent in the Corvette's structure troubled some staffers. "This car deserves to be as solid," commented executive editor Rich Ceppos, "as the Porsche 944s and Toyota Supra Turbos it trounces in performance."

McLellan's engineers were still working on that.

Top: *1988 brought the first all-new wheels to the Corvette since 1984. This convertible rides on the standard-equipment sixteen-inch units, while Z51 and Z52 Corvettes featured seventeen-inch rims with different cooling slots and flush covers over the hub and lug nuts. Bottom: The year 1988 brought another Corvette anniversary, and another anniversary edition Corvette. Available on the coupe only, the monochrome-white Thirty-fifth Anniversary package included the Z52 suspension, white leather seats, electronic climate control, a Delco-Bose stereo, and many other luxury touches.*

CHAPTER SEVEN

ZR-1 AND BEYOND

There is a price for glory, and it is high.
Brock Yates

Page 108: Chevrolet revived the LT1 engine designation for 1992. It was no empty promise: the significantly revised 350-cubic-inch V8 delivered 300 net horsepower, far more than the last of the emission-strangled LT1s in 1972. Page 109: The Corvette's crossed-flags emblem entered its fortieth year in 1992. Opposite page: The widened, convex rear end and square tail-lights first appeared on the limited run of ZR-1 prototypes built in 1989 and remained exclusive to the ZR-1 when this production model was built in 1990.

The Callaway Twin Turbo continued for 1988, now with 382 bhp, 562 pound-feet of torque, bigger brakes, and an available automatic transmission. Chevy sold 124 of them. But by late 1987 *Car and Driver* had already published "spy" photos of Chevrolet's own super-Corvette, to be powered by the four-cam Lotus LT5 V8, and GM vice president Lloyd Reuss had announced its existence at the Specialty Equipment Manufacturer's Association (SEMA) trade show in Las Vegas. In February 1988, *Road & Track* revealed that the $50,000 Corvette would be called ZR-1 (reviving the option code for the '71-'72 LT1 with competition suspension and cooling), that its engine would produce 370 bhp and 350 pound-feet of torque, and that it would ride on a basically stock suspension but with radically wider rear tires: 315/35ZR-17 Goodyear gatorbacks on eleven-inch rims.

To accommodate these rubber steamrollers, the designers widened the entire aft end of the car by three inches, flaring it out from around the middle of the doors. A unique rear fascia with square tail lamps further distinguished the ZR-1. *Car and Driver* expected it to be the "world's first 190-mph production sports car."

When the production ZR-1 appeared on *C/D*'s October 1988 cover, the editors captioned it "The Corvette from hell!" As expected, the Lotus engine shared only its 90-degree V8 configuration, 5.7-liter displacement, and 4.4-inch bore spacing with the Chevy small-block from which it was derived. Slightly smaller in bore and longer in stroke (3.90x3.66 inches), and boasting a titanic 11.3:1 compression ratio, the definitive LT5 produced 380 bhp at 6200 rpm and 370 pound-feet of torque at 4200 rpm. Topping the engine was a sixteen-runner intake manifold with sixteen separate fuel injectors. Solenoid-operated throttle plates blocked every other runner for better torque at low speed, and a separate three-stage throttle at the mouth of the plenum provided more delicate control of the beast within. Construction of the engine had been contracted to Mercury Marine in Oklahoma, and its exotic accessories included a water-cooled oil filter and a six-speed ZF transmission.

The six-speed was the only gearbox offered on the ZR-1, and it replaced the Doug Nash 4+3 on L98 Corvettes as well. But it hadn't entirely escaped computer control in the name of fuel efficiency. Chevrolet called the new system CAGS (for Computer Aided Gear Selection), and it locked out second and third gears when the engine was warm and the car was driven gently. *C/D*'s Csere thought the system felt "natural"; it handed you fourth when you reached for second, but the LT5 packed more than enough low-end grunt to overcome this handicap. Fifth and sixth were both overdrives; the latter was so tall it was essentially useless anywhere outside of the EPA's fuel-economy lab. (Were it not for air drag, the ZR-1 theoretically could have reached 306 mph without over-revving the engine.)

C/D first tested a ZR-1 in June. Editor William Jeanes commented that "it feels glued to the pavement, and it goes as if powered by equal parts lightning and rocket fuel." He found the Corvette chassis 100 percent up to the task of handling the power, calling it at once both "exciting and responsible." The magazine measured a 0 to 60 time of 4.5 seconds, a quarter mile in 12.8 at 111 mph, and a top speed of 175. And for all the transmission's CAGS assistance, Jeanes found it preferable to the Doug Nash 4+3.

Top: *The Corvette cruised in 1989 on standard equipment 17-inch alloy wheels. Changes under the skin included a six-speed manual transmission and an optional electronically controlled suspension.* **Bottom:** *In 1989 Callaway used the Sledgehammer—presumably named for the subtlety of its appearance—to test the company's aerodynamic modifications for the new-generation Corvette body. At 254.76 mph, this one-of-a-kind prototype shattered the track record at the Ohio Transportation Research Center.*

Best of all, Chevrolet engineers had finally tamed the Corvette's ride. Jeanes loved it. "Unlike previous Corvettes, the ZR-1 doesn't subject its drivers to corporal punishment....Twice, after driving hard all day on... roads that ranged from challenging to hostile, we emerged unscathed and unbrutalized by the ZR-1." The new Corvette, he concluded, "is the best thing yet seen from an American manufacturer." Chevrolet released a price of $51,500.

The engineers upgraded all '89 Corvettes with the Z52 suspension and structural improvements. The Z51 option remained, and a new FX3 package—available only with Z51—switched back to the base springs and added electronically adjustable shock absorbers. A console-mounted switch allowed the driver to select "touring," "sport," or "performance" programs for the shocks. All ZR-1s rode on the Z51/FX3 suspension, but with an even stiffer antiroll bar at the rear.

Also for 1989, ASC developed a steel-framed, fiberglass-skinned, removable hardtop for the convertible. Bolted in place, it gave the roadster 15 percent more torsional stiffness than the coupe, and met all federal roll-over standards for *fixed-roof* cars. "The extra rigidity provided by the hard top is something you can feel," noted *C/D* executive editor Ceppos, who was duly impressed with the Corvette Convertible's ever-growing civility. The L98 roadster sprinted to 60 mph in 5.8 seconds, spent only 14.4 seconds covering the quarter mile, and reached 142 mph with its hard roof in place.

Facing competition from the ZR-1, the Callaway Twin Turbo soldiered on, with more optional external vents and louvers to distinguish it from mere vacuum-breathing 'Vettes. In May 1989, *Car and Driver* measured a 0 to 60 time of 4.4 seconds and a quarter mile in 12.9 at 111 mph—about the same as the $20,000-cheaper ZR-1. No doubt the Callaway would have blown off the ZR-1 in a top-

speed contest, but *C/D*'s test car melted its turbochargers before it could prove it. The as-tested price had grown to $71,361, and model-year sales fell to sixty-nine.

Still, in 1989, Chevrolet sold sixty-nine more Callaways than ZR-1s. Bowling Green had built about one hundred '89 ZR-1's for the press and for its own evaluation. Then, in July, the company said it would delay public sales until a new interior was ready for all Corvettes in the fall.

The dash that came with that new 1990 interior, incorporating an uncomfortable combination of digital electronic and mechanical analog gauges, disappointed just about everyone. "The Corvette's cockpit may be improved, but it's still far from perfect," commented *Car and Driver* senior editor John Phillips III. "The hand brake remains between the driver and the door. The gargantuan rocker sills are still a major impediment to ingress and egress. The four ancillary analog gauges appear microscopically small...and the dark-orange

Handsome alloy wheels and unique ground-effects body work distinguish this 1990 Shinoda/Mears Edition Corvette. Larry Shinoda designed these after-market modifications, which became available to the public in 1992.

numerals atop the dull-gray instrument faces are difficult to decipher.'' Still, Phillips allowed that the new instrument panel represented an improvement over the ''exploding scoreboard'' it replaced.

The press welcomed the changes under the hood, where lighter pistons and an improved engine-control computer boosted the L98's horsepower to 250 at 4400 rpm and torque to 350 pound-feet at 3200 rpm—good, according to *C/D*, for 0 to 60 in 6 seconds flat and a quarter mile in 14.5 with a 3.33:1 rear.

At the Detroit Auto Show in March, Chevrolet presented a mid-engine, Corvette-badged prototype bearing the rather historically pregnant moniker of CERV-III. Having evolved directly from the Corvette Indy of 1986,

Right and below: By 1990, Callaway's twin-turbo Corvettes were producing 403 bhp, and were available in roadster as well as coupe configurations.

this apparent heir to CERVs I and II (the acronym now stood for Corporate Experimental Research Vehicle) featured all-wheel-drive and a turbocharged LT5 engine producing 650 bhp. To keep all this power on the ground, a central computer coordinated CERV-III's active suspension, active four-wheel steering, antilock brakes, and traction control.

All Corvettes entered 1991 with ZR-1–style convex rear bumpers and square taillamps—a change which surely displeased anyone who'd bought a '90 ZR-1 for its exclusive look. Up front, the Corvette gave up the last vestige of its visible air intake (filled with directional signals and fog lights since 1984) and instead sported a rounder bumper with wrap-around light clusters. Low on the side, the shark gills gave way to four horizontal strakes—recalling the nonfunctional air outlets of the 1963–64 models. A new exhaust system offered a slightly subdued sound, while even base Corvettes benefited from electronically controlled damping. The ZR-1 remained, of course, as *Car and Driver* said in April, ''a wild animal you can live with—barely.'' Its base price had risen to $64,138.

Meanwhile, the Detroit Auto Show saw the debut of the ZR-1 Spyder, a one-off silver bullet presented by Chevy management as a real possibility for production. Essentially a ZR-1 in convertible guise, its windshield ended at half of production height, fiberglass headrest farings blended the seats into the rear deck, and the deck itself spilled into the interior in a style reminiscent of the old solid-axle roadsters. The seats themselves mounted directly to the floorpan, so that under-six-footers, at least, could keep their eyeballs out of the airstream. Yellow-painted brake calipers echoed the striking neon yellow of the upholstery.

With 1992 came major revisions to the standard Corvette V8. All new induction parts—from the air cleaner through the ports—boosted airflow by 15 percent for better performance at high rpm. Reverse-flow cooling delivered cool water from the radiator directly to the heads, which in turn allowed 10.5:1 compression. Chevrolet dropped the L98 designation and revived the LT1 code. In this case, the tribute to the Corvette's muscular past was no empty promise; for the first time since 1970, the standard Corvette engine was rated 300 brake horsepower. In 1992, however, that number represented *net* brake horsepower. Even the original LT1 had delivered only 330 bhp *gross* in 1971, and 255 in 1972. Chevrolet claimed 0 to 60 in less than five seconds, and a top speed over 160 mph—both figures considerably better than the 6.0 seconds and 137 mph recorded for the original LT1 by *Car and Driver* in June 1971.

A ZR-1 from 1991, showing the new, rounded front bumper and wraparound light cluster. When you see this in your rear-view mirror, it's time to move over.

Above: Another Callaway variation, the Speedster, featured a unique cut-down windshield for a total height of just forty-one inches. By the winter of 1992–93, Callaway had completed ten twin-turbocharged Speedsters, and planned to build forty more with the new "Supernatural 475" power plant. Right: In 1990, this curvaceous new instrument panel replaced the doggedly rectilinear "exploding scoreboard" of 1984–89 and survived basically unchanged in the 1992 example shown here.

Backing up the new engine was a new traction control system called Acceleration Slip Regulation (ASR). In low-speed situations, like ice or snow, it selectively applied one or both rear brakes; at higher speeds it turned back the ignition timing and actually pushed back the accelerator pedal, so the driver knew when it was working—a feature first seen on CERV-III. A kill switch still allowed tire-melting takeoffs whenever the owner desired. The tires that would be melting were Goodyear Eagle GS-Cs, all-new, exclusive to the Corvette, and going for the record for asymmetry: not only were they unidirectional and asymmetric across the tread, but their tread block size changed around the circumference to reduce resonant road noise. More sound insulation, a retuned base suspension, and minor revisions to the instrument cluster completed the year's improvements.

Rich Ceppos, by then another of *Car and Driver's* editors-at-large, provided an interesting analogy, writing that the new '92 Corvette was "as fundamentally changed as a born-again Christian....The new 'Vette may possess the best ride of any sports car....Once a raw, rambunctious sports powerhouse, the Corvette seems on its way to becoming a sophisticated, all-weather, long-distance touring machine."

Later that year—on July 2, to be exact—Bowling Green rolled out the one-millionth Corvette. Appropriately enough, the factory finished the landmark roadster in white with a red interior and donated it to the nearby National Corvette Museum.

After the breathtaking improvements of 1992, the Corvette entered its fortieth anniversary year with only minor revisions. Chevrolet downsized the front wheels of the LT1 by one inch—to 8.5 inches, with 255/45ZR17 tires—while at the same time widening the rear tires to 285/40ZR17. This provided essentially the same ratio of rubber, front to rear, as the ZR-1 enjoyed. (Autocross-oriented Z07 models kept the 9.5-inch front rims.) A new camshaft gave the LT1 340 lb-ft of torque at 3600 rpm, while ported and polished heads boosted horsepower in the ZR-1 to 405, and torque to 385 lb-ft at 5200 rpm. There was another Anniversary Edition, of course, this time wearing Ruby Red metallic paint, red leather, and red wheel centers. Any Corvette—LT1 coupe, roadster, or ZR-1—could be dressed accordingly.

Bigger news arrived from the Callaway camp. After more or less sitting out 1992, the Connecticut tuner returned to 1993 with not one but two new Corvette engine packages—and not a turbocharger in sight. Reshaped ports and combustion chambers, a hotter cam, and appropriate tweaks for the engine computer wrung 400 bhp and 414 lb-ft of torque out of the LT1, while similar modifications (but using the stock cam-shafts) boosted the LT5 all the way to 475 bhp. These naturally aspirated hot-rods cost enormously less than the

old twin-turbocharger package with all its ancillary plumbing—just $10,390 plus an LT1, in fact, or $14,750 plus an LT5. Initially, Callaway called the modified engines "CL-1" and "CR-1" respectively, but quickly dropped the alphabet soup in favor of the more descriptive—and evocative—"Supernatural 400" and "Supernatural 475."

With the introduction of the 1993 version, however, the "new generation" Corvette had seen as many seasons as the original live-axle roadster—and twice as many as the Sting Ray that followed it. Ceppos had even commented, in his glowing review of the '92, that the Corvette was reaching an age "when most models are in the autumn of their years." Still, the late eighties and early nineties had brought very little of the Is-this-the-next-Corvette speculation that so preoccupied the press a decade before. Perhaps that was because the '84 model just wore a lot better than the '68.

The Corvette celebrated four decades of production with "Ruby Red" metallic paint, red leather, and red-accented wheel centers. The $1,455 package also included chrome 40th Anniversary badges on the hood, fenders, and fuel filler; plus matching embroidery on the headrests.

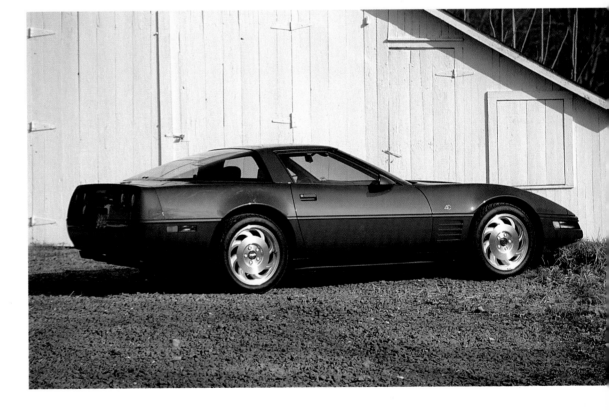

The General was working on a new Corvette nonetheless, and in July 1990, *Car and Driver* revealed that the company had targeted the summer of 1994 for its debut. Accompanying the article were studio photos—ostensibly unauthorized—of a clay model that Ceppos called "the leading design proposal for the new car." Proportioned similarly to the '84-generation 'Vette, but featuring rounder, more organic surfaces, the clay model clearly intended its engine to be installed in front of the driver. Its single most surprising feature, perhaps, was its exposed headlights. But then new lighting technology—in addition to significant reform of lighting regulations in the United States—had made it possible to integrate exposed lights into forms where they would previously have had to be hidden.

Ceppos' inside sources said a thirty-two-valve aluminum V8 displacing between 4.2 and 5.0 liters—and possibly supplied by Isuzu—would drive the rear wheels only. The Lotus-built LT5 would remain an option. The new 'Vette would probably incorporate CERV-III's active four-wheel steering and advanced traction control. Its body still would consist of fiberglass panels over a steel skeleton. As Ceppos wrote, "Tradition dies hard. The Chevy folks cherish their 35 years of building Corvettes from fiberglass."

But 1993 also saw Chevrolet losing sales and market share, not only to foreign competitors but to old arch-rival Ford as well. Scrambling to redesign bread-and-butter cars like the Cavalier and Lumina left few resources for developing an exotic new Corvette. *AutoWeek* reported on February 8 that Chevy had delayed the all-new Corvette until 1997, when a 5.7-liter Chevrolet engine would provide the power.

The one thing that remained certain was that the Corvette automobile would continue. And, of course, so would the controversy....

Pages 118–119: With the ZR-1's reputation firmly established, Chevrolet engineers turned their attention to the basic Corvette and the venerable small-block V8 that had survived since 1955. An all-new intake system, combined with 10.5:1 compression, produced an honest 300 net horsepower in the 1992 edition. With this new prowess came an old label: LT-1. Left: Callaway returned in 1993 with the "Supernatural 400," a thoroughly massaged but still atmospheric LT1 that delivered nearly the same horsepower as the old twin-turbo. For more serious speed addicts, Callaway also offered the Supernatural 475 shown here—a similarly tweaked ZR-1 producing 475 bhp. In addition to the Supernatural engines, Callaway offered four-piston Brembo brakes, a coil-spring suspension conversion, Connolly leather, custom wheels and paint, Bridgestone run-flat tires, and the essentially unchanged Aerobody kit, all offered à la carte, or together as an integrated package.

CHAPTER EIGHT

CONTENDERS TO THE THRONE

Make no mistake: horsepower covers

for a lot of sins.

Patrick Bedard

From *Car and Driver,* September 1990

"The penalty of leadership," according to an old Cadillac ad bearing that headline, is that everyone compares themselves to the leader. The Corvette quickly established itself as America's only sports car, which by default made it America's best sports car. So naturally the automotive press compared the Corvette to some of Europe's best sports cars—and to anything else the United States produced that claimed to be a sports car or even remotely resembled one.

It started even before the first Corvette reached the showroom. "Chevrolet and Kaiser-Frazer are racing to see which will be first on the market with a volume-produced American sports car," reported *Road & Track* in April 1953. "Chevrolet's Corvette will be powered by a souped-up engine delivering 160 bhp. K-F's car, designed by Howard Darrin, will be known as the DKF-161. Both will have fiberglass bodies, at least at first."

As time went on, the press used the Corvette more and more often as the yardstick against which any new contender in the automotive field was measured. This, perhaps, can be viewed as the highest possible tribute that could be paid to any automobile—even if the 'Vette didn't always come out on top.

Surprisingly, *Road & Track* road tested a Nash Healey in the same issue as its first-ever test of a Corvette, in June 1954, and not once did it draw a comparison between the two cars. If they had compared them, they would have noticed that the 'Vette, at two-thirds the list price ($3760 versus $6000), beat the Healey to 60 mph (11.0 versus 11.5 seconds) and equaled its performance in the quarter mile, where both cars scored eighteen seconds flat. And at 106.4 mph, the Corvette bettered the Healey's top speed by almost two mph.

Motor Trend, on the other hand, published the earliest Corvette versus Thunderbird comparison that same month—before Ford's two-seater had even reached its definitive design, much less production. Since no T-Bird was available for stopwatch timing, the comparison was somewhat limited, although Detroit editor Don MacDonald captured the two cars' differing philosophies when he wrote that "the Corvette was patterned closely after the European concept of a competition car. Conversely, the designers of the Thunderbird aimed at and achieved a California custom flavor."

Two years later, when *MT* clamped a fifth wheel on a real T-Bird and a somewhat more developed, eight-cylinder Corvette, the numbers turned out surprisingly close. Both cars sprinted to 60 in about 11½ seconds; the 'Bird cleared the quarter mile in 18.0 at 76.5 mph, the 'Vette in 17.9 at 77.5. But the Corvette beat the 'Bird handily for road grip and was easier to bring back into line once a slide had started. Interestingly, the difference in price between the two cars wouldn't buy your lunch, even then.

In 1957, *MT* compared the Corvette not only to the Thunderbird but also to the Studebaker Golden Hawk. "Acceleration is fierce," wrote author Wayne Thomas about the fuel-injected 'Vette, and indeed the Chevy ran away with the quarter-mile contest, finishing in 14.9 seconds at 95.0 mph. After driving all three, however, the editors wished for a single car that would combine "the instrumentation of the Golden Hawk, the cornering ability of the Corvette, and the detail finish of the Thunderbird."

The Ford-powered AC Cobra appeared in 1963 as the first serious rival to the Corvette—or at least the first one powered by a U.S. engine. "The Corvette has been

With its Stinger hood, side pipes, and alloy wheels, this looks like the ultimate '67 Corvette. Its only real domestic rival was the admittedly more useful—but slower—Shelby GT-500.

In compensation, the editors called the Corvette ''a completely civilized vehicle''—which could hardly be said about the Cobra.

But when *Motor Trend* matched a 427 Sting Ray against a different kind of snake in April 1967, it was the Corvette that looked uncivilized. Chevy's best easily outran the Shelby GT 500 in the quarter mile (13.8 seconds at 104 mph versus 14.5 at 101) and in top speed (143 mph vs. 120), and handled better too—whenever its skinnier tires could find some traction. Not surprisingly, however, *MT* judged the Mustang-based Shelby ''a more practical car for everyday use.''

In June 1969, *Road & Track* attempted to place the Corvette in the global order of things when it tested a base-engine, automatic transmission model against a Jaguar E-type, Mercedes-Benz 280 SL, and Porsche 911T. Our hero out-cornered all but the Porsche on the skid pad, trounced all but the Jag in the quarter mile, and at 132 mph simply ran away with the top-speed honors, a full 10 mph faster than the second-place Porsche. In subjective ratings of everything from appearance to visibility to braking and handling, however, the Corvette finished dead last. And in those days, at least, the financial distance between a 'Vette and a Jaguar or Porsche measured less than $1000.

Motor Trend reached a very different conclusion only one year later, when it tested an LT1 against a Porsche 911E. No one was surprised when the big Chevy V8 dominated the quarter-mile contest (14.4 seconds and 102 mph against 15.9 and 93), but when the Corvette outdistanced the Porsche around the Orange County Raceway, it raised some editorial eyebrows. Furthermore, the 'Vette cornered in flat, controllable drifts, while the 911E heeled over, hung on tight up to its limit, and then promptly spun into the weeds. And while the German car scored points for workmanship and interior

clouted from its position of absolute primacy in large-displacement, production-category racing,'' pronounced *Road & Track* that June. Smaller and lighter by half a ton, the 271-bhp Cobra clobbered even the fuel-injected Corvette in the quarter mile, reaching 113 mph in 13.8 seconds. (The Corvette took a second longer and didn't even reach 100.) And with about 16 percent less frontal area, the Cobra topped the 'Vette's 140-mph terminal velocity by a good 10 mph. In ride and handling, however, the Corvette's comparatively sophisticated suspension more than compensated for its greater bulk.

All that had changed by November 1965, when *Car and Driver* tested the totally redesigned Cobra 427. Applying the lessons Ford had learned with the GT-40 resulted in superb handling and braking for the Cobra. The seven-liter power plant could reel in a quarter mile of pavement in just 12.2 seconds at 118 mph, and didn't run out of breath until 165. The 427 Sting Ray tested in the same issue cost $1000 less and still managed to cover the comfort, the price had risen to $8,360—while the 'Vette sold for $6,333.

When the V12 Jaguar E-type appeared in 1971, *Motor Trend* found that the LT1 bettered it as well, with stronger acceleration (14.3 versus 14.8 seconds in the quarter), better road feel, and a generally more comfortable interior. "Despite Detroit's myopia and failures," editor Eric Dahlquist concluded, "they can still build one of the best cars anywhere, not for nine or ten grand, but six."

A few years after the demise of the Cobra, Ford tried again with a Dearborn-powered hybrid. In September 1973, when *MT* tested a DeTomaso Pantera and an LS4 Corvette at Ontario Motor Speedway, Zora Arkus-Duntov himself insisted on supervising the procedure. Despite overheating and fuel starvation in the corners, the Pantera lapped Ontario almost three mph faster than

Automobile buff books matched the original LT1 against some of Europe's finest machinery—with surprising results. In a 1970 **Motor Trend** *test, an LT1 turned faster lap times at California's Orange County Raceway than a more expensive Porsche 911E. A few months later,* **MT** *testers found that a 1971 LT1 like the one shown here outran, outhandled, and generally outclassed the new Jaguar E-Type V12.*

Despite increasing weight and decreasing horsepower, the 1976 Corvette could still outrun any other U.S. production car. Car and Driver *clocked a 'Vette at 124.5 mph that year—a significant 2.7 mph faster than the next closest contender, a 360-cubic-inch Dodge Dart Sport.*

the Plastic Fantastic, 129.68 mph versus 126.76. Then Zora asked the editors if *he* could drive the Corvette. He raised its average speed to 129.87, which no one could beat with the Pantera.

Malcolm Bricklin, on the other hand, insisted his Bricklin SV-1 was *not* intended to rival the Corvette, but as *MT* administrative editor Jim Brokaw wrote in May 1975, "there's only one other two-seater, plastic bodied sporty car in town." Actually, *Motor Trend* matched *two* Bricklins against an L48 Corvette: a 1974 model powered by an American Motors 360-cubic-inch V8, and a '75 Bricklin packing a 351 Ford. Mr. Bricklin's modesty aside, both SV-1s arrived at the end of the quarter mile ahead of the 'Vette—the AMC-powered car by nearly a second and 3 mph—and both handled more predictably. But both Bricklins lost points for their cramped, poorly designed, and abominably assembled interiors.

As the seventies progressed, testing the Corvette against just about anything else became a sort of national pastime—or at least a way to sell magazines in the terrible performance doldrums of that era. For its April 1976 issue, *Car and Driver* pitted an L82 'Vette against a motley collection of U.S. machinery in a top-speed contest at Troy Dry Lake in California. At 124.5 mph, the Corvette won the title of America's fastest production car. The only surprise was the second-place finisher, a 360-cubic-inch Dodge Dart Sport whose 121.8 mph edged out the third-place Pontiac Firebird Trans Am at 117.6. *C/D* performed a similar exercise at the Ohio Transportation Research Center in November 1977, this time inviting such imported notables as the Saab 99 Turbo, Mazda Cosmo, and Porsche 924. None could match the Corvette's much-improved 133.7 mph.

As the Corvette proved its dominance against American machinery, writers began to compare it more often to expensive, European exotics. In December 1979, three *Motor Trend* editors rendered their personal impressions of the Corvette L82, the Ferrari 308 GTS, and the Porsche 928. Senior editor Leon Mandel and editor-at-large Burge Hulett agreed that the Porsche was a pretty awful car for anything but top-speed runs, that the Ferrari was the most fun for an occasional night out, but that the Corvette would be easiest to live with. Associate editor Peter Frey disagreed; he couldn't come to terms with the 'Vette's numb steering and the time it took to settle on its suspension after every change in direction, and voted it dead last on the desirability list. (Hulett cited the same shortcomings, but seemed unfazed by them.) Nonetheless, the three cars finished close in timed performance tests. The Ferrari pranced quickest through the quarter-mile, followed by the 'Vette; the Porsche won the brake contest, again with the Chevy in second; and the Vette scored last in the lane change but first in the slalom. The bottom line, of course, was that the price of either the Porsche or the Ferrari would have bought *three* Corvettes.

When *Car and Driver* pitted a 'Vette against a 308 GTSi in November 1981, the editors also invited a Porsche 911SC, a Datsun 280-ZX Turbo, and a DeLorean DMC-12. The Corvette tied the Datsun in the quarter mile (15.4 seconds apiece), but both were beaten by the Porsche, and all but the DeLorean topped the 'Vette's 130-mph maximum speed. The Chevy fared best on the tight, smooth Waterford Hills road course in Michigan, where its 58.9-mph average bettered the second-place Ferrari's by almost 2 mph. But on a timed stretch of bumpy public pavement, where all five cars occasionally reached maximum velocity, the Corvette just couldn't keep up with its rivals from the continent, both of which averaged 82 mph. The Porsche, wrote associate editor Larry Griffin, "gave not a single damn how bad the road got," while the Ferrari "nonchalantly balanced across" the imperfect pavement. The stiffly-sprung Corvette tied the equally brutish Datsun for third (seventy-eight mph).

Chrome grilles and custom wheels brighten the familiar shape of this '81 Corvette.

Top: Sixteen separate intake runners and twin-cam heads distinguish the mighty LT5 power plant of the Corvette ZR-1. Even Acura's vaunted, aluminum-framed NSX couldn't beat the ultimate 'Vette in a quarter-mile contest—or in Road & Track's 700-foot slalom. Still, the R&T editors liked the Acura's "finesse." Bottom: A ZR-1 body meets the appropriate running gear in Bowling Green. Despite the car's potent performance, actual ZR-1 production never met GM's expectations.

Only the relatively underpowered DeLorean finished behind them.

In August 1983, *Road & Track* arranged a rematch between the all-new Corvette and the new Ferrari 308 GTBi Quattrovalvole—as well as Porsche's 944 and 928S. The Corvette had gotten better—but so had its rivals. The three eight-cylinder cars finished the quarter mile only a tenth of a second apart, but both the 308 and 928 were moving faster than the 'Vette, at 91.5 and 92.0 mph versus 87.5. The 'Vette's top end of 139 mph placed it behind the European V8s as well, although the plastic Chevy stopped shorter than even the lightweight 944. The 'Vette scored subjective points for acceleration and handling, and lost some for "its indecisive automatic transmission, overdone instrumentation, and various body rattles." The Ferrari and bigger Porsche cost twice as much, but the staff voted the 'Vette the least desirable, even considering its price.

The following January, *Road & Track* pitted the new 'Vette against the totally new Nissan 300-ZX Turbo. This turned out to be a very close match, but the 'Vette still squeaked ahead in acceleration, top speed, skid pad, and slalom, while losing the brake test by a yard. The Chevy also won friends for its clean, uncluttered styling. But several staffers noticed that the rougher the road, the less trouble the Nissan had keeping up with the Corvette, and they again voted the 'Vette the loser largely because of its ride.

A redesigned 300ZX Turbo returned for a rematch in *Car and Driver* in February 1990. Now the Nissan had the upper hand in speed (155 mph versus 148), and although it lost the skid pad contest it won decisively in the slalom. The acceleration contest was almost too close to call. In the subjective areas, the 'Vette swept the votes for performance and handling, but lost every category pertaining to comfort or practicality to its cheaper Japa-

nese competitor. ''The decisive uppercut,'' wrote senior editor John Phillips III, ''came out of the rising sun.''

Just as the L98 was showing its age, however, the ZR-1 arrived to carry the flag. Pitted against the Acura NSX and Porsche 911 Carrera 2 in the August 1990 *Road & Track,* the quad-cam Corvette proved itself fastest in the quarter mile, the skid pad, and the 700-foot slalom—even if it couldn't match the Acura's ''finesse.'' One month later, *Car and Driver* tested a ZR-1 against an NSX, a 911 Carrera 4, a Lotus Esprit Turbo SE, and a Ferrari 348ts. Here the 'Vette won the quarter mile and top-speed contests—the former by a hair, but the latter by a considerable margin—and finished second to the Ferrari on the skid pad, second to the Acura in braking, and third to the Acura and Porsche in the 1000-foot slalom. In the subjective categories, the editors voted it third overall.

''If only it didn't rattle and creak so much,'' explained editor-at-large Bedard. ''If only the instrument panel weren't so gauche.''

In *C/D*'s April 1991 issue, a $68,135 ZR-1 held off even a $105,191 Porsche 911 Turbo in the top speed contest, although the Porsche bettered the Corvette's 13.2 second quarter mile by nearly half a second. The 'Vette won the braking and slalom contests as well, and—at long last—the editor's subjective approval. ''The ZR-1 triumphed over the 911 Turbo for one simple reason,'' explained executive editor Rich Ceppos. ''It goes fast better.''

For sheer raw performance, the Corvette had equalled the best the world had to offer for nearly three decades. Now a silkier, more refined Corvette was ready to pose the question: Why *do* those imported exotics cost so much?

Having been tested against just about everything else the world had to offer, the ZR-1 remained "King of the Hill" in every objective measure of performance. This example dates from 1991.

CHAPTER NINE

CORVETTES THAT COULD HAVE BEEN

A class working hero is something to be.
Road & Track, October 1987

Page 132: The original Mako Shark II mock-up, with its finned and black-crackle-painted external exhausts. Working under Mitchell's direction, Larry Shinoda secretly developed this wild and wonderful creation in the GM Styling warehouse. Page 133: In 1960, Chevrolet designers added this double-bubble canopy with handy periscope to the flamboyant XP-700 roadster. Opposite page: Two of the three 1954 Motorama Corvettes. With its fixed roof, glass windows, and external door buttons, the fastback Corvair (top) nearly made it to production. The Nomad wagon (bottom) did see production, albeit in a somewhat modified form. Although it used some modified Corvette body panels, the show Nomad actually rode on a stock '53 Chevy sedan chassis. The mass-produced version bowed with the nose and modified quarter panels (with unique wheel openings) from the '55 Bel Air.

The Corvette began its public life as a Motorama show car, and it probably spawned more show cars and experimental prototypes than any other American production automobile. Some of them influenced future Corvettes, others were influenced by future Corvettes, and still others pointed down blind alleys. At least one, the spectacular Mako Shark II, virtually defined the auto-show special for an entire generation.

What follows is not a definitive listing of Corvette prototypes, but rather the selected highlights from forty years of original thinking. These are the Corvettes that might have been.

The auspicious Motorama debut of the original '53 roadster left Harley Earl's stylists reaching for an encore. After a great deal of brainstorming, they conceived three clever Corvette variations for the 1954 show, each designed to bless the 'Vette with increased comfort and utility, with minimal compromise to its sporty character. Two of the three, at least, would prove prophetic.

The first took a minimalist approach to transforming the Spartan roadster into a more civilized GT, adding roll-up windows, exterior door locks, and an airy, graceful, removable hardtop. Although its headlights were still deeply recessed, it dispensed with the competition-inspired stone guards. All of these changes, of course, appeared on the 1956 production car, whose removable top virtually copied that of the show special.

The second of the '54 Motorama cars took the GT theme one step further, with a fixed, fastback top and a less radical curve to the windshield. The persistent Corvair name appeared on this one, and Chevrolet man-

agement considered production until it occurred to them that they weren't selling any roadsters.

The last of the trio would achieve legendary status as the long-lost Waldorf Nomad. Clare MacKichan told Ludvigsen that he conceived the Nomad to "double-cross" the competition, explaining that "nobody would expect to see a wagon version of the Corvette." Stylists Carl Renner and Bob Cadaret brought the idea to life using modified Corvette body panels on a standard '53 Chevy sedan chassis. Earl watched the crowd at the Waldorf-Astoria, noting their wide-eyed admiration for the sporty wagon, and promptly phoned MacKichan with orders to develop a production version. Renner actually cut and spliced existing full-size drawings of the Nomad and the planned '55 Chevy and, somewhat remarkably, made the hybrid work. Chevrolet built 22,898 Nomads from 1955 to 1957—but as Bel Airs, not Corvettes.

In the summer of 1988, historian Mike Lamm reported in *Automobile Quarterly* that "two separate and independent sources" had assured him that the Waldorf Nomad remained stashed in a west coast warehouse. GM records say that the car was destroyed (as most show cars are) and the individual responsible for destroying it has confessed the deed on tape to the National Corvette Restorers Society. According to Lamm, however, a Washington-state Chevy dealer claims to have displayed the Nomad in his showroom weeks *after* the taped confession claims it was scrapped.

Interestingly, a shabby, olive-green Corvette professing to be the '54 Motorama hardtop showed up for sale at the Antique Automobile Club of America (AACA) national meet in Hershey, Pennsylvania, in October

1990. It had acquired more conventional door handles —and a 327 V8 with a four-speed—but otherwise played the part convincingly. The owner, refreshingly honest about the car's dubious past, admits he is still looking for absolute proof of its authenticity.

As the fifties progressed, Mitchell and Earl concentrated their styling energy on racing prototypes like the SR-2 and Corvette SS. Of course, the 1957 AMA resolution against racing changed all that.

Mitchell's XP-700, built in the summer of 1958 but not shown publicly until some time later, never raced—but it ran, having been built on a production fuel-injected chassis. *Motor Trend* thought that the bubble-topped car "appears as though it should be orbiting the earth," but the magazine was observant enough to point out that Mitchell had borrowed the XP-700's "floating grille"

and clear-glass headlights from California customizer George Barris. *MT* predicted that the XP-700's rear-view periscope "would shortly find its way from idea cars to production." It was this car that inspired *Sports Cars Illustrated*'s daring prediction of an all-new, possibly steel-bodied Corvette for 1960. Of course, only the XP-700's pert little tail saw production, on the face-lifted Corvette of 1961 and 1962.

The first of Mitchell's Shark cars debuted at Road America in Elkhart Lake, Wisconsin, in June 1961. By that time Mitchell had virtually completed (though not yet won approval for) the 1963 Sting Ray, and wanted—for his own satisfaction as much as anything—to test the limits of the new design. A few years ago, Larry Shinoda described Mitchell's instructions to *Road & Track* editor-at-large John Lamm: Take the Sting Ray design and

Bill Mitchell's XP-700 inspired all kinds of rumors when it first appeared in public in 1959. Actually, its aft end accurately predicted that of the '61–'62 Corvettes. A more subtle detail, its "floating grille," inspired dozens of similar designs during the next decade.

Another view of the XP-700. Its "floating grille" inspired dozens of similar designs during the next decade, while its divided rear window predicted a similar feature on the '63 Sting Ray coupe.

With the deliberately outrageous 1961 Shark, Mitchell tested the extremes of the Sting Ray styling theme. Some of its more extravagant details included marker lights housed in its forward-facing fish gills and mirrored flaps that popped up from the rear deck to reflect the horizontally mounted turn signals. The wood-rimmed steering wheel that complimented its original interior had been a gift to Mitchell from Enzo Ferrari.

"keep doing it until I say ouch." This Shinoda did, even specifying a grille that resembled the mesh of shark teeth. Mitchell wanted the car painted to match the shark in his office, fading from blue-black on top to a light gray at the bottom. When the boys in the paint shop couldn't match the car to the fish to Mitchell's satisfaction, reported Shinoda, they secretly repainted the fish to match the car. "You guys really captured it," exclaimed the very pleased Design vice president, who apparently never figured out exactly how they had done it.

The Shark evolved over the years, its supercharged 327 replaced by a normally aspirated ZL1 big block, and its stock '61 dashboard by a wood-grain, European-style panel that looked altogether too tame. GM renamed it Mako Shark in 1965, when it toured the show circuit with Shinoda's even more radical Mako Shark II.

The Mako Shark II that debuted at the New York Auto Show in the spring of 1965 was only a mockup. It would have been difficult to drive anyway, with its funky, squared-off steering handle (one could hardly call it a "wheel") that incorporated thumb-wheels for turn signals and gear selection. GM built a working version later that year, with a radically revised interior and without external exhausts. The color contrast between top and bottom was more sudden and striking on the running car, which was powered by a 427 cubic-inch V8. (Emblems on the mockup had announced a 396 under the hood.) The working Mako Shark II debuted at the Paris Auto Show in October 1965, toured Europe, and returned for the New York Auto Show in 1966. A bank of computers behind the seats managed the neon-tube instrument display, a curious foreshadowing of the '84 dashboard. Then, with a revised, tunneled backlight, and yet another variation on the familiar paint scheme, the running Mako II became the 1969 Manta Ray. Mitchell eventually acquired it for his own collection, along with the original Shark and the Sting Ray racer.

One of the most interesting Corvette experimentals, the XP-819, actually originated outside Duntov's Corvette group, in Chevrolet Research and Development under engineer Frank Winchell. Winchell's experiments with high-performance Corvairs had convinced him that a rear-engine Corvette might be possible, and he probed the limits of the idea with an unlikely, backbone-framed vehicle whose all-aluminum, 287-cubic-inch V8 hung out behind its rear axle. Shinoda designed the body in the Mako Shark mold, and the whole fiberglass-skinned creation was merrily sliding backward off the test track by early 1965. Bunkie Knudsen, then Chevrolet general manager, sent the unruly would-be 'Vette to race-car builder Smokey Yunick for dismantling. Yunick cut the chassis in half but stashed the pieces in a paint booth, figuring he'd use them some day in chassis experiments of his own. This he did, eventually, and with about as much success as Winchell. In 1976, a Corvette enthusiast bought the remains and had them restored. The original engine had vanished long ago, however, and the XP-819 now appears at occasional Corvette shows toting a cast-iron 327 in its tail.

By 1971, Mitchell's staff had totally re-bodied one of the three XP-882 chassis originally built for the 1970 mid-engine prototype discussed in Chapter 4, giving it rounder, softer ends in anticipation of federal bumper standards. Their revisions also included round headlight covers (à la Opel GT), a tunneled rear window, and the new designation XP-895. Ludvigsen said that Chevrolet general manager John DeLorean influenced some of these changes, and then arranged with Reynolds Metals to duplicate the car in aluminum. The resulting aluminum unibody saved about 500 pounds and would have anticipated the Acura NSX by nearly two decades. But DeLorean couldn't justify the cost of production.

GM's brief flirtation with the Wankel rotary engine led to two of the most famous Corvette show cars of the seventies. Mitchell thought that a smaller, mid-engine Corvette, powered by a compact rotary engine, might

replace both the contemporary Corvette and the Opel GT. MacKichan, by then chief of Advanced Design, headed the project, which began in early 1971 and came to be known as XP-897GT. He picked the Dino 246GT as his target for size and proportion. Designers Dick Finegan and Otto Soeding penned the actual shape, which both derived from and improved on the aluminum-bodied XP-895. To complete the car in time for a new-product presentation to the board of directors in June 1972, "Mac" arranged for Italian coachbuilder Pininfarina to construct the body on a Porsche 914 chassis that Duntov's staff had shortened and otherwise modified. Pininfarina finished the rotary Corvette in time, but the car somehow missed the board meeting anyway and didn't make its public debut until the Frankfurt Auto Show in September 1973.

In the winter of 1971-72, with the Italians working feverishly to complete XP-897GT, Duntov decided to

Another view of the first Mako Shark II. Its unusual features included electrically powered, retractable stabilizing flaps and a flip-top roof. Concealed windshield wipers and door handles, and later concealed bumpers and an electronic dashboard, appeared on production Corvettes.

design a big-block version. He assigned his assistant, Gib Hufstader, the task of mating *two* of the experimental rotary engines together—for a total of four rotors and 585 cubic inches—in another of the XP-882 chassis, still using the existing, modified E-body drivetrain. It was an incredibly complex task, but Hufstader completed it in only two months.

Styling the car proved equally complicated. Mitchell believed that the widely copied Kamm tail of the production Corvette had grown stale and clichéd, and wanted to experiment with gently tapered rear ends, like those of the Mercedes-Benz and Auto Union Grand Prix cars of the thirties. The trouble was, as Dr. Kamm had pointed out back then, that tapered tails only look aerodynamic; unless they are made impractically long, they actually increase lift and drag by increasing the surface area exposed to turbulent air flow. Henry Haga, who then headed Chevrolet Studio Three, knew this, and the conflict between aerodynamics and aesthetics led to at least one explosive argument with Mitchell.

According to John Lamm (who, incidentally, is not related to Mike Lamm), Haga finally gave in. "Unless we try it and can say we've tried it," the studio chief told Jerry Palmer, then his assistant, "we can't say it doesn't work." They developed a double-ended body, based on the 1970 show car but more graceful, with folding gullwing doors. Paul Bracq, then BMW's design chief, told *Road & Track* European correspondent Paul Frère that the four-rotor Corvette was the most brilliantly designed car he had seen for a long time.

The four-rotor Corvette returned for one more season on the show circuit; Mitchell rescued it from storage in 1975, installed a 400-cubic-inch Chevrolet small block, and renamed it the Aerovette. General Motors still has the car.

Tamer show cars dominated the late seventies and early eighties, as the automakers devoted their design and engineering resources to developing smaller, more efficient products. Late in 1979 GM showed the press the Turbo Corvette, an engineering exercise that wrung some-

Another descendant of the XP-882, the 1973 Corvette four-rotor reflected Mitchell's fascination with thirties-era streamlining. Mitchell later installed a 400-cubic-inch V8 and renamed it the Aerovette.

where between 260 and 290 bhp from the L48 engine using fuel injection and turbocharging. Only minor trim changes, however, distinguished the prototype from production 'Vettes that breathed at atmospheric levels. "There's enough all-American low-end torque to give you a nosebleed," reported *Car and Driver* technical editor Don Sherman. Interestingly, the Turbo Corvette's throttle plate lived *upstream* of the turbocharger, and while the car carried no emissions hardware, it was all so well planned and well finished that Sherman thought it must have been destined for production. But the project never saw the light of day again.

The 1986 Corvette Indy, mentioned briefly in Chapter 6, marked the renaissance of the show-car spectacular. Palmer designed it, although he credits Design staffers Tom Peters for the initial rendering and Tom Reiss for the clay sculpturing. The British Ilmore company supplied its 2.6-liter V8 engine, the same powerplant that Chevrolet sponsors in a number of British March chassis for the U.S. Championship Auto Racing Teams (CART) series and also, of course, for the Indianapolis 500. Converted to conventional fuel for the show car, the twin-cam, twin-turbocharged unit still produced some 600 bhp. Four-wheel drive, active suspension, active four-wheel-steering, and traction control would help all that power reach the pavement safely. Except that the Corvette Indy was only a mockup; GM contracted Lotus to build a running prototype, which evolved into the CERV-III of 1990.

Curiously, while Corvette engineers profess their faith in the conventional front-engine layout, *all* of the significant Corvette show cars of the last two decades have carried their powerplants behind the seats. Obviously, the mid-engine vision lives on at General Motors.

We may yet see the 'Vette Duntov wanted within his lifetime.

Jerry Palmer broke a ten-year lull in show-Corvette activity when he sprung the Corvette Indy on the world in 1986. Its electronically controlled throttle, all-wheel drive, and all-wheel steering have since appeared on various production sports cars, but not on the Corvette.

APPENDIX I

Specifications, Prices, and Production, 1953–93

All prices include freight. The dimensions and weights given here apply to the base model unless otherwise noted; production figures apply to the model year. Accurate sales information on engine options is not available before 1964.

From 1981 on, the ninth digit of each Corvette serial number was calculated by plugging the final six digits into a closely guarded formula; this made it more difficult for thieves to counterfeit Corvette serial plates.

1953

Available Engines	"Blue Flame" Six
Displacement, cu. in.	235
Bore, in.	3⁹/₁₆
Stroke, in.	3¹⁵/₁₆
Compression	8.0:1
Bhp @ rpm	150 @ 4200
Fuel delivery	3x1 bbl

Dimensions & Weight

Wheelbase, in.	102.0	Height, in.	52.1
Length, in.	167.0	Weight, lb.	2850.0
Width, in.	72.2	Weight distrib., f/r	53/47

Production	Base Price	Serial Numbers
Roadster 300	$3498	E53F001001-001300

1954

Available Engines	"Blue Flame" Six
Displacement, cu. in.	235
Bore, in.	3⁹/₁₆
Stroke, in.	3¹⁵/₁₆
Compression	8.0:1
Bhp @ rpm	155 @ 4200
Fuel delivery	3x1 bbl

Dimensions & Weight

Wheelbase, in.	102.0	Height, in.	52.1
Length, in.	167.0	Weight, lb.	2850.0
Width, in.	72.2	Weight distrib., f/r	53/47

Production	Base Price	Serial Numbers
Roadster 3640	$2952	E54S001001-004640

1955

Available Engines	"Blue Flame" Six	V8
Displacement, cu. in.	235	265
Bore, in.	3⁹/₁₆	3³/₄
Stroke, in.	3¹⁵/₁₆	3
Compression	8.0:1	8.0:1
Bhp @ rpm	155 @ 4200	195 @ 5000
Fuel delivery	3x1 bbl	1x4 bbl

Dimensions & Weight

Wheelbase, in.	102.0	Height, in.	52.1
Length, in.	167.0	Weight, lb.	2850.0
Width, in.	72.2	Weight distrib., f/r	53/47

Production	Base Price	Serial Numbers
Roadster 700	$2774	*VE55S001001-001700

*Delete "V" for six-cylinder cars.

1956

Available Engines	Base V8	RPO469
Displacement, cu. in.	265	265
Bore, in.	3³/₄	3³/₄
Stroke, in.	3	3
Compression	9.25:1	9.25:1
Bhp @ rpm	210 @ 5200	225 @ 5200
Fuel delivery	1x4 bbl	2x4 bbl

Dimensions & Weight

Wheelbase, in.	102.0	Height, in.	52.0
Length, in.	168.0	Weight, lb.	2880.0
Width, in.	70.5	Weight distrib., f/r	52/48

Production	Base Price	Serial Numbers
Convertible 3467	$2900	E56S001001-004467

1957

Available Engines	Base V8	RPO469A	RPO579A	RPO469B	RPO579B/E*
Displacement, cu. in.	283	283	283	283	283
Bore, in.	3⁷/₈	3⁷/₈	3⁷/₈	3⁷/₈	3⁷/₈
Stroke, in.	3	3	3	3	3
Compression	9.5:1	9.5:1	9.5:1	9.5:1	10.5:1
Bhp @ rpm	220 @ 4800	245 @ 5000	250 @ 5000	270 @ 6000	290 @ 6200
Fuel delivery	1x4 bbl	2x4 bbl	port inj.	2x4 bbl	port inj.

*RPO579E has cold-air induction.

Dimensions & Weight

Wheelbase, in.	102.0	Height, in.	52.0
Length, in.	168.0	Weight, lb.	2880.0
Width, in.	70.5	Weight distrib., f/r	52/48

Production	Base Price	Serial Numbers
Convertible 6339	$3176	E57S100001-106339

1958

Available Engines	Base V8	RPO469	RPO579	RPO469C	RPO579D
Displacement, cu. in.	283	283	283	283	283
Bore, in.	$3^7/8$	$3^7/8$	$3^7/8$	$3^7/8$	$3^7/8$
Stroke, in.	3	3	3	3	3
Compression	9.5:1	9.5:1	9.5:1	9.5:1	10.5:1
Bhp @ rpm	230 @ 4800	245 @ 5000	250 @ 5000	270 @ 6000	290 @ 6200
Fuel delivery	1x4 bbl	2x4 bbl	port inj.	2x4 bbl	port inj.

Dimensions & Weight

Wheelbase, in.	102.0	Height, in.	52.4
Length, in.	177.2	Weight, lb.	3080.0
Width, in.	72.8	Weight distrib., f/r	53/47

Production	Base Price	Serial Numbers
Convertible 9168	$3591	J58S100001-109168

1959

Available Engines	Base V8	RPO469	RPO579	RPO469C	RPO579D
Displacement, cu. in.	283	283	283	283	283
Bore, in.	$3^7/8$	$3^7/8$	$3^7/8$	$3^7/8$	$3^7/8$
Stroke, in.	3	3	3	3	3
Compression	9.5:1	9.5:1	9.5:1	9.5:1	10.5:1
Bhp @ rpm	230 @ 4800	245 @ 5000	250 @ 5000	270 @ 6000	290 @ 6200
Fuel delivery	1x4 bbl	2x4 bbl	port inj.	2x4 bbl	port inj.

Dimensions & Weight

Wheelbase, in.	102.0	Height, in.	52.4
Length, in.	177.2	Weight, lb.	3080.0
Width, in.	72.8	Weight distrib., f/r	53/47

Production	Base Price	Serial Numbers
Convertible 9670	$3875	J59S100001-109670

1960

Available Engines	Base V8	RPO469	RPO469C	RPO579*	RPO579D*
Displacement, cu. in.	283	283	283	283	283
Bore, in.	$3^7/8$	$3^7/8$	$3^7/8$	$3^7/8$	$3^7/8$
Stroke, in.	3	3	3	3	3
Compression	9.5:1	9.5:1	9.5:1	11.0:1	11.0:1
Bhp @ rpm	230 @ 4800	245 @ 5000	270 @ 6000	275 @ 5200	315 @ 6200
Fuel delivery	1x4 bbl	2x4 bbl	2x4 bbl	port inj.	port inj.

*Because of casting problems with their aluminum heads, engines 579 and 579D reverted to 1958-59 specifications in March 1960.

Dimensions & Weight

Wheelbase, in.	102.0	Height, in.	52.4
Length, in.	177.2	Weight, lb.	3080.0
Width, in.	72.8	Weight distrib., f/r	53/47

Production	Base Price	Serial Numbers
Convertible 10,261	$3872	00867S100001-110261

1961

Available Engines	Base V8	RPO469	RPO468	RPO353	RPO354
Displacement, cu. in.	283	283	283	283	283
Bore, in.	$3^7/8$	$3^7/8$	$3^7/8$	$3^7/8$	$3^7/8$
Stroke, in.	3	3	3	3	3
Compression	9.5:1	9.5:1	9.5:1	11.0:1	11.0:1
Bhp @ rpm	230 @ 4800	245 @ 5000	270 @ 6000	275 @ 5200	315 @ 6200
Fuel delivery	1x4 bbl	2x4 bbl	2x4 bbl	port inj.	port inj.

Dimensions & Weight

Wheelbase, in.	102.0	Height, in.	52.2
Length, in.	176.7	Weight, lb.	3035.0
Width, in.	70.4	Weight distrib., f/r	53/47

Production	Base Price	Serial Numbers
Convertible 10,939	$3934	10867S100001-110939

1962

Available Engines	Base V8	RPO583	RPO396	RPO582
Displacement, cu. in.	327	327	327	327
Bore, in.	4	4	4	4
Stroke, in.	$3^1/4$	$3^1/4$	$3^1/4$	$3^1/4$
Compression	10.5:1	10.5:1	11.25:1	11.25:1
Bhp @ rpm	250 @ 4400	300 @ 5000	340 @ 6000	360 @ 6000
Fuel delivery	1x4 bbl	1x4 bbl	1x4 bbl	port inj.

Dimensions & Weight

Wheelbase, in.	102.0	Height, in.	52.2
Length, in.	176.7	Weight, lb.	3065.0
Width, in.	70.4	Weight distrib., f/r	53/47

Production	Base Price	Serial Numbers
Convertible 14,531	$4038	20867S100001-114531

1963

Available Engines	Base V8	L75	L76	L84
Displacement, cu. in.	327	327	327	327
Bore, in.	4	4	4	4
Stroke, in.	$3^1/4$	$3^1/4$	$3^1/4$	$3^1/4$
Compression	10.5:1	10.5:1	11.25:1	11.25:1
Bhp @ rpm	250 @ 4400	300 @ 5000	340 @ 6000	360 @ 6000
Fuel delivery	1x4 bbl	1x4 bbl	1x4 bbl	port inj.

Dimensions & Weight

Wheelbase, in.	98.0	Height, in.	49.6
Length, in.	175.2	Weight, lb.	3130.0
Width, in.	69.2	Weight distrib., f/r	48/52

Production		Base Price	Serial Numbers
Coupe	10,594	$4257	30837S100001-121513
Convertible	10,919	$4037	30867...

1964

Available Engines

	Base V8	L75	L76	L84
Displacement, cu. in.	327	327	327	327
Bore, in.	4	4	4	4
Stroke, in.	3¼	3¼	3¼	3¼
Compression	10.5:1	10.5:1	11.25:1	11.25:1
Bhp @ rpm	250 @ 4400	300 @ 5000	365 @ 6200	375 @ 6200
Fuel delivery	1x4 bbl	1x4 bbl	1x4 bbl	port inj.
Number sold	3262	10,471	7171	1325

Dimensions & Weight

Wheelbase, in.	98.0	Height, in.	49.6
Length, in.	175.2	Weight, lb.	3130.0
Width, in.	69.2	Weight distrib., f/r	48/52

Production | **Base Price** | **Serial Numbers**
Coupe 8,304	$4252	40837S100001-122229
Convertible 13,925	$4037	40867...

1965

Available Engines

	Base V8	L75	L79	L76	L84	L78
Displacement, cu. in.	327	327	327	327	327	396
Bore, in.	4	4	4	4	4	4³/₃₂
Stroke, in.	3¼	3¼	3¼	3¼	3¼	3⁴⁹/₆₄
Compression	10.5:1	10.5:1	11.0:1	11.25:1	11.25:1	11.0:1
Bhp @ rpm	250 @ 4400	300 @ 5000	350 @ 5800	365 @ 6200	375 @ 6200	425 @ 6400
Fuel delivery	1x4 bbl	1x4 bbl	1x4 bbl	1x4 bbl	port inj.	1x4 bbl
Number sold	2609	8358	4716	5011	771	2157

Dimensions & Weight

Wheelbase, in.	98.0	Height, in.	49.8
Length, in.	175.1	Weight, lb.	3130.0
Width, in.	69.6	Weight distrib., f/r	48/52

Production | **Base Price** | **Serial Numbers**
Coupe 8,186	$4321	194375S100001-123562
Convertible 15,376	$4106	19467...

1966

Available Engines

	Base V8	L79	L36	L72
Displacement, cu. in.	327	327	427	427
Bore, in.	4	4	4¼	4¼
Stroke, in.	3¼	3¼	3⁴⁹/₆₄	3⁴⁹/₆₄
Compression	10.5:1	11.0:1	10.25:1	11.0:1
Bhp @ rpm	300 @ 5000	350 @ 5800	390 @ 5400	425 @ 6400
Fuel delivery	1x4 bbl	1x4 bbl	1x4 bbl	1x4 bbl
Number built	9755	7591	5116	5258

Dimensions & Weight

Wheelbase, in.	98.0	Height, in.	49.8
Length, in.	175.1	Weight, lb.	3130.0
Width, in.	69.6	Weight distrib., f/r	48/52

Production | **Base Price** | **Serial Numbers**
Coupe 9,958	$4295	194376S100001-127720
Convertible 17,762	$4084	19467...

1967

Available Engines

	Base V8	L79	L36	L68	L71	L88
Displacement, cu. in.	327	327	427	427	427	427
Bore, in.	4	4	4¼	4¼	4¼	4¼
Stroke, in.	3¼	3¼	3⁴⁹/₆₄	3⁴⁹/₆₄	3⁴⁹/₆₄	3⁴⁹/₆₄
Compression	10.5:1	11.0:1	10.25:1	10.25:1	11.0:1	12.5:1
Bhp @ rpm	300 @ 5000	350 @ 5800	390 @ 5400	400 @ 5400	435 @ 5800	560 @ 6400
Fuel delivery	1x4 bbl	1x4 bbl	1x4 bbl	3x2 bbl	3x2 bbl	1x4 bbl
Number sold	6842	6375	3832	2101	3770*	20

*Includes 16 aluminum-head L89s.

Dimensions & Weight

Wheelbase, in.	98.0	Height, in.	49.8
Length, in.	175.1	Weight, lb.	3130.0
Width, in.	69.6	Weight distrib., f/r	48/52

Production | **Base Price** | **Serial Numbers**
Coupe 8,504	$4389	194377S100001-122940
Convertible 14,436	$4241	19467...

1968

Available Engines

	Base V8	L79	L36	L68	L71	L88
Displacement, cu. in.	327	327	427	427	427	427
Bore, in.	4	4	4¼	4¼	4¼	4¼
Stroke, in.	3¼	3¼	3⁴⁹/₆₄	3⁴⁹/₆₄	3⁴⁹/₆₄	3⁴⁹/₆₄
Compression	10.5:1	11.0:1	10.25:1	10.25:1	11.0:1	12.5:1
Bhp @ rpm	300 @ 5000	350 @ 5800	390 @ 5400	400 @ 5400	435 @ 5800	560 @ 6400
Fuel delivery	1x4 bbl	1x4 bbl	1x4 bbl	3x2 bbl	3x2 bbl	1x4 bbl
Number sold	5875	9440	7717	1932	3522*	80

*Includes 624 aluminum-head L89s.

Dimensions & Weight

Wheelbase, in.	98.0	Height, in.	47.0
Length, in.	182.5	Weight, lb.	3210.0
Width, in.	69.0	Weight distrib., f/r	49/51

Production | **Base Price** | **Serial Numbers**
Coupe 9,936	$4663	194378S400001-428566
Convertible 18,630	$4320	19467...

1969

Available Engines	Base V8	L46	L36	L68	L71	L88
Displacement, cu. in.	350	350	427	427	427	427
Bore, in.	4	4	4$^{1}/_{4}$	4$^{1}/_{4}$	4$^{1}/_{4}$	4$^{1}/_{4}$
Stroke, in.	3$^{31}/_{64}$	3$^{31}/_{64}$	3$^{49}/_{64}$	3$^{49}/_{64}$	3$^{49}/_{64}$	3$^{49}/_{64}$
Compression	10.25:1	11.0:1	10.25:1	10.25:1	11.0:1	12.5:1
Bhp @ rpm	300 @ 4800	350 @ 5600	390 @ 5400	400 @ 5400	435 @ 5800	560 @ 6400
Fuel delivery	1x4 bbl	1x4 bbl	1x4 bbl	3x2 bbl	3x2 bbl	1x4 bbl
Number sold	10,083	12,846	10,531	2072	3112*	118**

*Includes 390 aluminum-head L89s.
**Includes 2 aluminum-block ZL1s.

Dimensions & Weight

Wheelbase, in.	98.0	Height, in.	47.8
Length, in.	182.5	Weight, lb.	3210.0
Width, in.	69.0	Weight distrib., f/r	49/51

Production		Base Price	Serial Numbers
Coupe	22,129	$4781	194379S700001-738762
Convertible	16,633	$4438	19467...

1970

Available Engines	Base V8	L46	LT1	LS5	LS7
Displacement, cu. in.	350	350	350	454	454
Bore, in.	4	4	4	4$^{1}/_{4}$	4$^{1}/_{4}$
Stroke, in.	3$^{31}/_{64}$	3$^{31}/_{64}$	3$^{31}/_{64}$	4	4
Compression	10.25:1	11.0:1	11.0:1	10.25:1	12.25:1
Bhp @ rpm	300 @ 4800	350 @ 5600	370 @ 6000	390 @ 4800	465 @ 5200
Fuel delivery	1x4 bbl	1x4 bbl	1x4 bbl	1x4 bbl	1x4 bbl
Number sold	6646	4910	1287	4473	0

Dimensions & Weight

Wheelbase, in.	98.0	Height, in.	47.8
Length, in.	182.5	Weight, lb.	3280.0
Width, in.	69.0	Weight distrib., f/r	49/51

Production		Base Price	Serial Numbers
Coupe	10,668	$5192	194370S400001-417316
Convertible	6,648	$4849	19467...

1971

Available Engines	L48	LT1	LS5	LS6
Displacement, cu. in.	350	350	454	454
Bore, in.	4	4	4$^{1}/_{4}$	4$^{1}/_{4}$
Stroke, in.	3$^{31}/_{64}$	3$^{31}/_{64}$	4	4
Compression	8.5:1	9.0:1	8.5:1	9.0:1
Bhp @ rpm	270 @ 4800	330 @ 5600	365 @ 4800	425 @ 5600
Fuel delivery	1x4 bbl	1x4 bbl	1x4 bbl	1x4 bbl
Number sold	14,547	1957*	5097	200**

*Includes 8 ZR1s with competition radiator, transmission, suspension, brakes.
**Includes 12 ZR2s with competition radiator, transmission, suspension, brakes.

Dimensions & Weight

Wheelbase, in.	98.0	Height, in.	47.8
Length, in.	182.5	Weight, lb.	3280.0
Width, in.	69.0	Weight distrib., f/r	49/51

Production		Base Price	Serial Numbers
Coupe	14,680	$5496	194371S100001-121801
Convertible	7,121	$5259	19467...

1972

Available Engines	L48	LT1	LS5
Displacement, cu. in.	350	350	454
Bore, in.	4	4	4$^{1}/_{4}$
Stroke, in.	3$^{31}/_{64}$	3$^{31}/_{64}$	4
Compression	8.5:1	9.0:1	8.5:1
Bhp @ rpm	200 @ 4400	255 @ 5600	270 @ 4000
Fuel delivery	1x4 bbl	1x4 bbl	1x4 bbl
Number sold	21,330	1761*	3913

*Includes 20 ZR1s with competition radiator, transmission, suspension, brakes.

Dimensions & Weight

Wheelbase, in.	98.0	Height, in.	47.8
Length, in.	182.5	Weight, lb.	3280.0
Width, in.	69.0	Weight distrib., f/r	49/51

Production		Base Price	Serial Numbers
Coupe	20,496	$5533	1Z37[K,L,V,W*]2S500001-527004
Convertible	6,508	$5296	1Z67...

*K = L48, L = LT1, V or W = LS5

1973

Available Engines	L48	L82	LS4
Displacement, cu. in.	350	350	454
Bore, in.	4	4	4¼
Stroke, in.	3³¹/₆₄	3³¹/₆₄	4
Compression	8.5:1	9.0:1	8.25:1
Bhp @ rpm	190 @ 4400	250 @ 5200	275 @ 4000
Fuel delivery	1x4 bbl	1x4 bbl	1x4 bbl
Number sold	20,342	5710	4412

Dimensions & Weight

Wheelbase, in.	98.0	Height, in.	47.8
Length, in.	184.7	Weight, lb.	3407.0
Width, in.	69.0	Weight distrib., f/r	49/51

Production		Base Price	Serial Numbers
Coupe	25,521	$5562	1Z37[J,T,Z*]3S400001-434464**
Convertible	4,943	$5398	1Z67...

*J = L48, T = L82, Z = LS4.
**No cars were built with serial numbers 24001 through 28000.

1974

Available Engines	L48	L82	LS4
Displacement, cu. in.	350	350	454
Bore, in.	4	4	4¼
Stroke, in.	3³¹/₆₄	3³¹/₆₄	4
Compression	8.5:1	9.0:1	8.25:1
Bhp @ rpm	195 @ 4400	250 @ 5200	270 @ 4000
Fuel delivery	1x4 bbl	1x4 bbl	1x4 bbl
Number sold	27,318	6690	3494

Dimensions & Weight

Wheelbase, in.	98.0	Height, in.	48.0
Length, in.	185.5	Weight, lb.	3390.0
Width, in.	69.0	Weight distrib., f/r	49/51

Production		Base Price	Serial Numbers
Coupe	32,028	$6002	1Z37[J,T,Z*]4S400001-437502
Convertible	5,474	$5766	1Z67...

*J = L48, T = L82, Z = LS4.

1975

Available Engines	L48	L82
Displacement, cu. in.	350	350
Bore, in.	4	4
Stroke, in.	3³¹/₆₄	3³¹/₆₄
Compression	8.5:1	9.0:1
Bhp @ rpm	165 @ 3800	205 @ 4800
Fuel delivery	1x4 bbl	1x4 bbl
Number sold	36,093	2372

Dimensions & Weight

Wheelbase, in.	98.0	Height, in.	48.0
Length, in.	185.2	Weight, lb.	3530.0
Width, in.	69.0	Weight distrib., f/r	48/52

Production		Base Price	Serial Numbers
Coupe	33,836	$6810	1Z37[J,T*]5S400001-438465
Convertible	4,629	$6550	1Z67...

*J = L48, T = L82.

1976

Available Engines	L48	L82
Displacement, cu. in.	350	350
Bore, in.	4	4
Stroke, in.	3³¹/₆₄	3³¹/₆₄
Compression	8.5:1	9.0:1
Bhp @ rpm	180 @ 4000	210 @ 5200
Fuel delivery	1x4 bbl	1x4 bbl
Number sold	40,838	5720

Dimensions & Weight

Wheelbase, in.	98.0	Height, in.	48.0
Length, in.	185.2	Weight, lb.	3530.0
Width, in.	69.0	Weight distrib., f/r	48/52

Production		Base Price	Serial Numbers
Coupe	46,558	$7605	1Z37[L,X*]6S400001-446558

*L = L48, X = L82.

1977

Available Engines

	L48	L82
Displacement, cu. in.	350	350
Bore, in.	4	4
Stroke, in.	3³¹/₆₄	3³¹/₆₄
Compression	8.5:1	9.0:1
Bhp @ rpm	180 @ 4000	210 @ 5200
Fuel delivery	1x4 bbl	1x4 bbl
Number sold	43,065	6148

Dimensions & Weight

Wheelbase, in.	98.0	Height, in.	48.0
Length, in.	185.2	Weight, lb.	3534.0
Width, in.	69.0	Weight distrib., f/r	48/52

Production | **Base Price** | **Serial Numbers**
Coupe 49,213 | $8648 | 1Z37[L,X*]7S400001-449213

*L = L48, X = L82.

1978

Available Engines

	L48	L82
Displacement, cu. in.	350	350
Bore, in.	4	4
Stroke, in.	3³¹/₆₄	3³¹/₆₄
Compression	8.2:1	9.0:1
Bhp @ rpm	185 @ 4000	220 @ 5200
Fuel delivery	1x4 bbl	1x4 bbl
Number sold	34,037	12,739

Dimensions & Weight

Wheelbase, in.	98.0	Height, in.	48.0
Length, in.	185.2	Weight, lb.	3495.0
Width, in.	69.0	Weight distrib., f/r	47/53

Production | **Base Price** | **Serial Numbers**
Coupe 40,274 | $9,352 | 1Z87[L,4*]8S400001-440274
Pace Car 6,502 | $13,653 | 1Z87[L,4*]8S900001-906502

*L = L48, 4 = L82.

1979

Available Engines

	L48	L82
Displacement, cu. in.	350	350
Bore, in.	4	4
Stroke, in.	3³¹/₆₄	3³¹/₆₄
Compression	8.2:1	9.0:1
Bhp @ rpm	195 @ 4000	225 @ 5200
Fuel delivery	1x4 bbl	1x4 bbl
Number sold	39,291	14,516

Dimensions & Weight

Wheelbase, in.	98.0	Height, in.	48.0
Length, in.	185.2	Weight, lb.	3655.0
Width, in.	69.0	Weight distrib., f/r	48/52

Production | **Base Price** | **Serial Numbers**
Coupe 53,807 | $10,220 | 1Z87[8,4*]9S400001-453807

*8 = L48, 4 = L82.

1980

Available Engines

	LG4	L48	L82
Displacement, cu. in.	305	350	350
Bore, in.	3⁴⁷/₆₄	4	4
Stroke, in.	3³¹/₆₄	3³¹/₆₄	3³¹/₆₄
Compression	8.6:1	8.2:1	9.0:1
Bhp @ rpm	180 @ 4200	190 @ 4400	230 @ 5200
Fuel delivery	1x4 bbl	1x4 bbl	1x4 bbl
Number sold	3,221	32,324	5,069

Dimensions & Weight

Wheelbase, in.	98.0	Height, in.	48.1
Length, in.	185.3	Weight, lb.	3334.0
Width, in.	69.0	Weight distrib., f/r	48/52

Production | **Base Price** | **Serial Numbers**
Coupe 40,614 | $13,140 | 1Z87[8,6,H*]AS400001-440614

*8 = L48, 4 = L82, H = LG4 (required in California).

1981

Available Engines — **L81**
Displacement, cu. in.	350
Bore, in.	4
Stroke, in.	3³¹/₆₄
Compression	8.2:1
Bhp @ rpm	190 @ 4200
Fuel delivery	1x4 bbl

Dimensions & Weight
Wheelbase, in.	98.0	Height, in.	48.1
Length, in.	185.3	Weight, lb.	3282.0
Width, in.	69.0	Weight distrib., f/r	48/52

Production	Base Price	Serial Numbers
St. Louis 31,611	$16,259	1G1AY8764*BS400001-431611
Bowling Green 8,995	$16,259	1G1AY8764*B5100001-108995

*Ninth digit varies.

1982
(sold through February 1983)

Available Engines — **L83**
Displacement, cu. in.	350
Bore, in.	4
Stroke, in.	3³¹/₆₄
Compression	9.0:1
Bhp @ rpm	200 @ 5200
Fuel delivery	throttle-body inj.

Dimensions & Weight
Wheelbase, in.	98.0	Height, in.	48.1
Length, in.	185.3	Weight, lb.	3345.0
Width, in.	69.0	Weight distrib., f/r	46/54

Production	Base Price	Serial Numbers
Coupe 18,648	$18,290	1G1AY8786*C5100001-125407
Collector Ed. 6,759	$22,538	1G1AY078…

*Ninth digit varies.

1984
(first sold in March 1983)

Available Engines — **L98**
Displacement, cu. in.	350
Bore, in.	4
Stroke, in.	3³¹/₆₄
Compression	9.0:1
Bhp @ rpm	205 @ 4300
Fuel delivery	throttle-body inj.

Dimensions & Weight
Wheelbase, in.	96.2	Height, in.	46.7
Length, in.	176.5	Weight, lb.	3117.0
Width, in.	71.0	Weight distrib., f/r	51/49

Production	Base Price	Serial Numbers
Coupe 51,547	$21,800	1G1AY0781*E5100001-151477

*Ninth digit varies.

1985

Available Engines — **L98**
Displacement, cu. in.	350
Bore, in.	4
Stroke, in.	3³¹/₆₄
Compression	9.0:1
Bhp @ rpm	230 @ 4000
Fuel delivery	port inj.

Dimensions & Weight
Wheelbase, in.	96.2	Height, in.	46.7
Length, in.	176.5	Weight, lb.	3225.0
Width, in.	71.0	Weight distrib., f/r	51/49

Production	Base Price	Serial Numbers
Coupe 39,729	$24,891	1G1YY0787*F5100001-139729

*Ninth digit varies.

1986

Available Engines		L98	
Displacement, cu. in.		350	
Bore, in.		4	
Stroke, in.		3³¹/₆₄	
Compression		9.0:1*	
Bhp @ rpm		230 @ 4000	
Fuel delivery		port inj.	

*9.5:1 with aluminum heads on convertible.

Dimensions & Weight

Wheelbase, in.	96.2	Height, in.	46.7
Length, in.	176.5	Weight, lb.	3190.0
Width, in.	71.0	Weight distrib., f/r	51/49

Production		Base Price	Serial Numbers
Coupe	27,794	$27,502	1G1YY0789*G5100001-127794
Convertible	7,315	$32,507	1G1YY678…

*Ninth digit varies.

1987

Available Engines		L98	B2K**
Displacement, cu. in.		350	350
Bore, in.		4	4
Stroke, in.		3³¹/₆₄	3³¹/₆₄
Compression		9.5:1	7.5:1
Bhp @ rpm		240 @ 4000	345 @ 4000
Fuel delivery		port inj.	port inj; twin turbo
Number sold		30,448	184

Dimensions & Weight

Wheelbase, in.	96.2	Height, in.	46.7
Length, in.	176.5	Weight, lb.	3216.0
Width, in.	71.0	Weight distrib., f/r	51/49

Production		Base Price	Serial Numbers
Coupe	20,007	$27,999	1G1YY2182*H5100001-130632
Convertible	10,625	$33,172	1G1YY318…

*Ninth digit varies.
**Although Callaway Engineering performed the actual conversion, Chevrolet offered the twin turbo-charged engine as factory option B2K.

1988

Available Engines		L98	B2K
Displacement, cu. in.		350	350
Bore, in.		4	4
Stroke, in.		3³¹/₆₄	3³¹/₆₄
Compression		9.5:1	7.5:1
Bhp @ rpm		240 @ 4000*	382 @ 4250
Fuel delivery		port inj.	port inj; twin turbo
Number sold		22,665	124

*245 @ 4300 in coupes with 3.07:1 axle.

Dimensions & Weight

Wheelbase, in.	96.2	Height, in.	46.7
Length, in.	176.5	Weight, lb.	3233.0
Width, in.	71.0	Weight distrib., f/r	51/49

Production		Base Price	Serial Numbers
Coupe	15,382	$29,955	1G1YY2182*J5100001-122789
Convertible	7,407	$35,295	1G1YY318…

*Ninth digit varies.

1989

Available Engines	L98	LT5	B2K
Displacement, cu. in.	350	350	350
Bore, in.	4	3⁹/₁₀	4
Stroke, in.	3³¹/₆₄	3⁶⁶/₁₀₀	3³¹/₆₄
Compression	9.5:1	11.0:1	7.5:1
Bhp @ rpm	240 @ 4000*	380 @ 6200	382 @ 4250
Fuel delivery	port inj.	port inj.	port inj; twin turbo
Number sold	26,343	0	69

*245 @ 4300 in coupes with 3.07:1 axle

Dimensions & Weight

Wheelbase, in.	96.2	Height, in.	46.7
Length, in.	176.5	Weight, lb.	3229.0
Width, in.	71.0	Weight distrib., f/r	51/49

Production		Base Price	Serial Numbers
Coupe	16,663	$32,045	1G1YY2186*K5100001-126412
Convertible	9,749	$37,285	1G1YY318…

*Ninth digit varies.

1990

Available Engines	L98	LT5	B2K
Displacement, cu. in.	350	350	350
Bore, in.	4	3⁹/10	4
Stroke, in.	3³¹/64	3⁶⁶/100	3³¹/64
Compression	9.5:1	11.0:1	7.5:1
Bhp @ rpm	245 @ 4000*	375 @ 5800	390 @ 4250
Fuel delivery	port inj.	port inj.	port inj; twin turbo
Number sold	20,547	3049	50

*250 @ 4400 in coupes with 3.07:1 axle and convertibles with 2.73:1 axle.

Dimensions & Weight

Wheelbase, in.	96.2	Height, in.	46.7
Length, in.	176.5	Weight, lb.	3223.0
Width, in.	71.0	Weight distrib., f/r	51/49

Production		Base Price	Serial Numbers
Coupe	12,967	$32,479	1G1YY2386*L5100001-123646
Convertible	7,630	$37,764	1G1YY3386*L51...
ZR-1	3,049	$59,495	1G1YZ23J6*L58...

*Ninth digit varies.

1991

Available Engines	L98	LT5	B2K
Displacement, cu. in.	350	350	350
Bore, in.	4	3⁹/10	4
Stroke, in.	3³¹/64	3⁶⁶/100	3³¹/64
Compression	10.0:1	11.0:1	7.5:1
Bhp @ rpm	245 @ 4000*	375 @ 5800	403 @ 4500
Fuel delivery	port inj.	port inj.	port inj; twin turbo
Number sold	18,532	2044	63

*250 @ 4400 in coupes with 3.07:1 and convertibles with 2.73:1 axle.
**Estimated at press time.

Dimensions & Weight

Wheelbase, in.	96.2	Height, in.	46.7
Length, in.	178.5	Weight, lb.	3223.0
Width, in.	71.1	Weight distrib., f/r	51/49

Production		Base Price	Serial Numbers
Coupe	12,923	$32,985	1G1YY2385*M5100001-120639
Convertible	5,672	$39,300	1G1YY3385*M51...
ZR-1	2,044	$64,668	1G1YZ23J5*M58...

*Ninth digit varies.

1992

Available Engines	LT1	LT5
Displacement, cu. in.	350	350
Bore, in.	4	3⁹/10
Stroke, in.	3³¹/64	3⁶⁶/100
Compression	10.5:1	11.0:1
Bhp @ rpm	300 @ 5000	375 @ 5800
Fuel delivery	port inj.	port inj.
Number sold	19,997	502

Dimensions & Weight

Wheelbase, in.	96.2	Height, in.	46.3
Length, in.	178.5	Weight, lb.	3223.0
Width, in.	71.1	Weight distrib., f/r	51/49

Production		Base Price	Serial Numbers
Coupe	14,102	$34,185	1G1YY23P4*N5100001-120479
Convertible	5,875	$40,695	1G1YY33P4*N51...
ZR-1	502	$65,868	1G1YZ23J4*N58...

*Ninth digit varies.

1993

Available Engines	LT1	LT5	SUPER 400***	SUPER 475***
Displacement, cu. in.	350	350	350	350
Bore, in.	4	3⁹/10	4	3⁹/10
Stroke, in.	3³¹/64	3⁶⁶/100	3³¹/64	3⁶⁶/100
Compression	10.5:1	11.0:1	10.5:1	11.0:1
Bhp @ rpm	300 @ 5000	405 @ 5800	400 @ 5800	475 @7000
Fuel delivery	port inj.	port inj.	port inj.	port inj.

Dimensions & Weight

Wheelbase, in.	96.2	Height, in.	46.3
Length, in.	178.5	Weight, lb.	3333
Width, in.	70.7	Weight distrib., f/r	51/49

Production	Base Price	Serial Numbers
Coupe**	$34,595	1G1YY23P*P5100001
Convertible**	$41,195	1G1YY33P*P51...
ZR-1**	$66,278	1G1YZ23J*P51...

*Ninth digit varies.
**Information not yet available.
***Chevrolet did not assign a factory option number to Callaway's ''Supernatural 400'' and ''Supernatural 475.'' However, many Chevrolet dealers continued to offer these modified Corvettes to their customers.

APPENDIX II

Corvettes in Competition

Since 1956, at least, Corvettes have competed in nearly every class of racing devised by humankind, from drag racing and speed trials to road racing, rallying, and Autocross. Indeed, the subject of Corvette racing could easily fill another book as large or larger than this one. The victories (and near victories) listed here merely highlight the Corvette's distinguished career in motor sports.

1956
First in class and ninth overall at 12 Hours of Sebring
SCCA C-Production National Champion

1957
First in class at 12 Hours of Sebring
SCCA B-Production National Champion
SCCA B-Sports National Champion

1958
First in GT category at 12 Hours of Sebring
First in class at Pikes Peak Hill Climb
SCCA B-Production National Champion

1959
SCCA B-Production National Champion

1960
Eighth overall at 24 Hours of LeMans
First in class at 12 Hours of Sebring
SCCA C-Sports Racing National Champion
SCCA B-Production National Champion

1961
First in GT category at 12 Hours of Sebring
First in class at Pikes Peak Hill Climb
SCCA B-Production National Champion

1962
First in class at Daytona Continental
First overall at 3 Hours of Riverside
SCCA A-Production National Champion
SCCA B-Production National Champion

1963
First in Prototype class at Nassau Trophy Race
SCCA B-Production National Champion

1964
First in GT category at 12 Hours of Sebring
First in GT category at Daytona Continental
SCCA B-Production National Champion

1965
First in class at 12 Hours of Sebring

1966
First in GT category at 12 Hours of Sebring
First in GT category at Daytona Continental

1967
First in GT category at 12 Hours of Sebring

1968
First in GT category at 12 Hours of Sebring
First in GT category at Daytona Continental

1969
First in class at Daytona Continental
First in GT category at Watkins Glen
    6 Hours of Endurance
Fourth in GT category at 1,000 Km
    of Spa-Francorchamps

SCCA A-Production National Champion
SCCA B-Production National Champion

1970
First in GT category at 12 Hours of Sebring
First in GT category at Daytona Continental
SCCA A-Production National Champion
SCCA B-Production National Champion

1971
First in GT category and fourth overall at
    24 Hours of Daytona
First in GT category at 12 Hours of Sebring
First in GT category at Watkins Glen
    6 Hours of Endurance
IMSA GT Manufacturers Champion
SCCA A-Production National Champion
SCCA B-Production National Champion

1972
First in GT category and fourth overall at
    24 Hours of Daytona
First in GT category at 12 Hours of Sebring
First in GTO category at Daytona Starlight
    3 Hour
IMSA GT Manufacturers Champion
SCCA A-Production National Champion
SCCA B-Production National Champion

1973
Second overall in Daytona Continental
SCCA B-Production National Champion
SCCA B-Stock Solo II National Champion
SCCA B-Prepared Solo II National Champion

1974
First overall in IMSA GT race at Daytona
First overall in IMSA GT race at Talladega
SCCA A-Production National Champion
SCCA B-Production National Champion
SCCA B-Stock Solo II National Champion

1975
First overall in IMSA GT finale at Daytona
First in class at Watkins Glen 6 Hours of
  Endurance
SCCA Trans-Am Series Champion
SCCA A-Production National Champion

1976
First in class at Daytona Continental
SCCA A-Production National Champion
SCCA B-Production National Champion
SCCA B-Stock Solo II National Champion

1977
SCCA A-Production National Champion
SCCA B-Stock Solo II National Champion
SCCA B-Prepared Solo II National Champion

1978
SCCA Trans-Am Series Category II Champion
IMSA AAGT Manufacturers Champion
SCCA A-Production National Champion
SCCA B-Production National Champion
SCCA B-Stock Solo II National Champion
SCCA B-Prepared Solo II National Champion
SCCA B-Stock Ladies Solo II National
  Champion

1979
SCCA Trans-Am Series Category I Champion
SCCA B-Production National Champion
SCCA B-Stock Solo II National Champion
SCCA B-Prepared Solo II National Champion
SCCA B-Stock Ladies Solo II National
  Champion

1980
SCCA Trans-Am Series Runner-Up
Two GTO class victories in IMSA

1981
SCCA Trans-Am Series Champion

1982
SCCA Trans-Am Series runner-up
One GTO class victory in IMSA

1984
SCCA Showroom Stock GT National
  Champion

1985
First in all six SCCA Showroom Stock
  Endurance Series races
SCCA Showroom Stock GT National
  Champion

1987
First in all seven SCCA Showroom Stock
  Endurance Series races
SCCA Showroom Stock GT National
  Champion*

1988
IMSA GTO Series runner-up

1990
Set new 5000km World Endurance Record of
  175.710 mph
Set new 5000-mile World Endurance Record
  of 173.791 mph
Set new 24-Hour World Endurance Record of
  175.885 mph
SCCA World Challenge Series Drivers
  Champion
SCCA World Challenge Series Team
  Champion
SCCA World Challenge Series Manufacturers
  Champion

1991
SCCA World Challenge Series Drivers
  Champion
SCCA World Challenge Series Team
  Champion
SCCA World Challenge Series Manufacturers
  Champion

1992**
SCCA World Challenge Series Drivers
  Champion
SCCA World Challenge Series Team
  Champion

*After this performance, the SCCA ruled that
the Corvette was too fast for the Showroom
Stock GT series and banned it from
competition in that class.
**SCCA did not award a Manufacturers
Champion in 1992.

APPENDIX III
Corvette Clubs

British Columbia Corvette Club
P.O. Box 20508
Burnaby, B.C.
Canada V5H 3X9

Corvette Club of America
P.O. Box 30223
Washington, DC 20814

Corvette Club of Ontario
P.O. Box 1065
Adelaide Street
Toronto, Ontario
Canada M5C 2K4

International Registry of Early Corvettes
P.O. Box 666
Corvalis, OR 97339

National Corvette Owners Association
900 South Washington Street
Falls Church, VA 22046

National Corvette Restorers Society
6291 Day Road
Cincinnati, OH 45247

National Council of Corvette Clubs
P.O. Box 325
Troy, OH 45373

'Vettes de Montreal
6600 St. Urbain
Ste. 304
Montreal, Quebec
Canada H2S 3G8

BIBLIOGRAPHY

Books

Antonick, Michael. *The Genuine Corvette Black Book*. Powell, Ohio: Michael Bruce Associates, Inc., 1990.

Consumer Guide Automobile Book 1989. Lincolnwood, Illinois: Publications International, Ltd., 1988.

Consumer Guide Automobile Book 1990. Lincolnwood, Illinois: Publications International, Ltd., 1989.

Consumer Guide Auto '91. Lincolnwood, Illinois: Publications International, Ltd., 1990.

Fenster, Julie M., ed. *Corvette: The Legend Lives On*. Newport Beach, California: CBS Inc., 1987.

Gunnell, John A., ed. *Standard Catalog of American Cars 1946-1975*. Iola, Wisconsin: Krause Publications, 1987.

Ludvigsen, Karl. *Corvette: America's Star Spangled Sports Car*. Princeton, NJ: Princeton Publishing, 1978.

Mitchell, William L., and Allan Girdler. *Corvette: A Piece of the Action*. Princeton, NJ: Princeton Publishing, 1984.

Paddock, Lowell C., ed. *Corvette: An American Legend*. Princeton, NJ: Princeton Publishing, 1986.

Road & Track on Corvette: 1953-67. Newport Beach, California: CBS Inc., 1984.

Periodicals
Automobile Quarterly

"Corvette Renaissance." John F. Katz. Vol. 24, No. 3, pp. 324-33.
"A Shark is not a Grouper: A Personal Profile of Bill Mitchell." Strother MacMinn. Vol. 26, No. 2, pp. 130–141.
"Where Are They Now?" Michael Lamm. Vol. 26, No. 3, pp. 270-89.

AutoWeek

"Escape Road: 1964 Chevrolet XP-819." Mike Mueller. Sep. 17, 1990, p. 60.

"And the Tradition Continues." John M. Clor. Nov. 16, 1992, p. 22.

"Turbos? We Don't Need No Stinking Turbos." Mark Vaughn. Jan. 25, 1993, pp. 16-18.

"Worth Their Wait in Gold?" Wes Raynal. Feb. 8, 1993, pp. 15–16.

Car and Driver

"Top of the Chevy Line: the Corvette Sting Ray." Oct. 1962, pp. 30-33.

"Mr. Corvette and His Cars." Jan P. Norbye. Nov. 1962, pp. 41-44.

"Corvette Sting Ray." May 1963, pp. 36-41.

"Corvette Sting Ray." Jan. 1965, pp. 42-44.

"Cobra 427." Nov. 1965, pp. 37-40, 76.

"Corvette Sting Ray 427." Nov. 1965, pp. 49-52.

"Eye-Opener." Dec. 1965, p. 74.

"Chevrolet Corvette 427." May 1967, pp. 53-56, 124-25.

"Chevrolet Corvette." Dec. 1967, p. 43.

"Corvette 427 Coupe." May 1968, pp. 47-50.

"Chevrolet Corvette Coupe." Sep. 1969, pp. 38-44.

"The Corvette Test." June 1971, pp. 28-33, 90-92.

"The '73 Corvette." July 1972, p. 36.

"1973 Corvette Comparison Test." Dec. 1972, pp. 34-39.

"1974 Corvette." Aug. 1973, p. 74.

"1976 Corvette?" David Abrahamson. Mar. 1975, p. 68.

"North to Alaska." Brock Yates. Feb. 1976, pp. 26-31, 72-74.

"Northwest Passage." Brock Yates. Mar. 1976, pp. 46-49, 72.

"Building the Yukon Corvette." Jim Williams. Mar. 1976, pp. 53-55, 75-76.

"Finding the Fastest American Car." Don Sherman. Apr. 1976, pp. 30-38, 82-84.

"Chevrolet Corvette." Patrick Bedard. Mar. 1977, p. 37.

"Chevrolet Corvette." Brock Yates. Oct. 1977, pp. 31-36.

"Flat-Out in Ohio!" Don Sherman. Nov. 1977, pp. 40-61.

"Chevrolet Corvette." Don Sherman. Dec. 1978, pp. 33-39.

"Future Shock from Chevy." Don Sherman. Dec. 1978, pp. 41-42.

"Seven Hundred Miles on Seven Cylinders." Don Sherman. Dec. 1978, pp. 45-49.

"The Corvette as Indy Pace Car." Rich Taylor. Dec. 1978, pp. 53-54.

"In Search of the Best-Handling American Car." Don Sherman. Sep. 1979, pp. 51-61.

"Turbo Titillations, Chevrolet Division." Don Sherman. Sep. 1979, pp. 63-66.

"Chevrolet Corvette." Patrick Bedard. May 1980, pp. 57-64.

"Sports-Car Showdown." Larry Griffin. Dec. 1981, pp. 39-47.

"Corvette Communique." Rich Ceppos and Jean Lindamood. Jan. 1982, p. 21.

"Last-of-Their-Kind-Corvettes." Don Sherman. Mar. 1982, pp. 47-55.

"Corvette!" Brock Yates. Mar. 1983, pp. 35-39.

"One Classy Chassis." Don Sherman. Mar. 1983, pp. 40-44.

"Design Staff's Dream Car." Jean Lindamood. Mar. 1983, pp. 45-49.

"The Buck Stops Here." John Hilton. Mar. 1983, pp. 51-53.

"Looking Backward." Michael Jordan. Mar. 1983, pp. 55-58.

"Spied! 1990 Corvette!" Arthur St. Antoine. June 1987, p. 33.

"Vette Variations." Csaba Csere. June 1987, pp. 109-13.

"Charting the Changes." Arthur St. Antoine. Oct. 1987, p. 49.

"Royal Vette!" Arthur St. Antoine. Nov. 1987, p. 31.

"Chevrolet Corvette." Csaba Csere. May 1988, pp. 44-51.

"Chevrolet Corvette ZR-1." Csaba Csere. Oct. 1988, pp. 38-42.

"Callaway Twin-Turbo Corvette." Rich Ceppos. May 1989, pp. 50-57.

"Chevrolet Corvette ZR-1." William Jeanes. June 1989, pp. 48-53.

"The Marque of Zora." Pete Lyons. June 1989, pp. 60-70.

"Chevrolet Corvette Convertible." Rich Ceppos. June 1989, pp. 74-76.

"For Your Information." Bill Visnic. July 1989, p. 25.

"Charting the Changes." Bill Visnic. Oct. 1989, p. 48.

"Comparison Test: Knockouts." John Phillips III. Feb. 1990, pp. 36-43.

"Chevrolet Corvette ZR-1." Rich Ceppos. Apr. 1990, pp. 57-62.

"Corvette Calculations." Rich Ceppos. July 1990.

"Comparison Test: The Eroticars." Patrick Bedard. Sep. 1990, pp. 42-57.

"Charting the Changes." Phil Berg. Oct. 1990, p. 55.

"Predators." Rich Ceppos. Apr. 1991, pp. 42-52.

"Corvette ZR-1 Spyder." Dick Kelly. Sep. 1991, p. 144.

"Charting the Changes." Phil Berg. Oct. 1991, pp. 34-40.

"Technical Highlights." Don Schroeder. Oct. 1991, pp. 44-47.

"Chevrolet Corvette." Rich Ceppos. Oct. 1991, p. 71.

"Charting the Changes." Phil Berg. Oct. 1992, p. 49.

Motor Trend

"Spotlight on Detroit." Floyd G. Lawrence. Sep. 1953, p. 10.

"From Dies to Driveway." Walt Woron. Sep. 1953, pp. 34-37.

"New Fuel for an Old Duel." Don MacDonald. June 1954, pp. 15-18, 62.

"'56 Thunderbird and Corvette Road Test." Walt Woron. June 1956, pp. 37-40.

"Corvette." Jan. 1957, pp. 28-29.

"More Detroit Sports Cars?" Wayne Thomas. Aug. 1957, pp. 18-21.

"Corvette." Joe H. Wherry. Dec. 1957, pp. 54-55, 60.

"XP-700: Tomorrow's Corvette?" July 1960, pp. 26-28.

"Corvette." Nov. 1960, pp. 62-63.

"Bred to Race." Roger Huntington. Jan. 1963, pp. 40-43, 94-95.

"Corvette Sting Ray." Jim Wright. May 1963, pp. 22-27.

"Corvette." Nov. 1963, p. 90.

"Corvette Sting Ray Road Test." Bob McVay. Sep. 1964, pp. 34-39.

"Corvette." Nov. 1964, p. 61.

"Mako Shark II." July 1965, pp. 66-67.

"Corvette." Nov. 1965, p. 39.

"Corvette." July 1966, pp. 28-29.

"Chevrolet Corvette." Nov. 1966, p. 39.

"Shelby GT 500 & 427 Sting Ray." Steve Kelly. Apr. 1967, pp. 24-29.

"The '68s Are Here: Chevrolet." Oct. 1967, pp. 72-73.

"Chevy's Heavy Lightweight." Eric Dahlquist. Sep. 1968, pp. 48-51.

"Inside Detroit." Dec. 1968, p. 10.

"The 1970 'Vette." Eric Dahlquist. Mar. 1970, pp. 88-89.

"The Great Corvette-Porsche Controversy." Chuck Koch. May 1970, pp. 76-78, 116.

"Mid-engine Corvette. What else?" Eric Dahlquist. June 1970, pp. 56-59, 114.

"Jaguar XKE V12 vs. Corvette LT-1 V8." Eric Dahlquist. Apr. 1971, pp. 36-38.

"The Glass Menagerie." Chuck Koch. June 1972, pp. 30-34, 136-37.

"Looking Back." June 1972, pp. 35, 126.

"International Report." Wally Wyss. Oct. 1972, pp. 23-26.

"Corvette Owner's Survey." Kyle Given. Jan. 1973, pp. 44-48.

"1st Photo of New 'Vette." Aug. 1973, p. 30.

"Pantera Versus Corvette." Jim Brokaw. Sep. 1973, pp. 76-78.

"Corvette and Bricklin, Camaro and Firebird." Jim Brokaw. May 1975, pp. 92-100.

"Corvette '77." Tony Swan. Dec. 1976, pp. 34-38.

"Survivor 'Vette." Tony Swan. Dec. 1976, pp. 40-42.

"Aero-Vette." Bob Hall. Dec. 1976, pp. 44-47.

"The Shape of 'Vettes to Come." Dec. 1976, pp. 49-50.

"Corvette, Everyman's Sports Car." Dec. 1977, pp. 51-56.

"Silver Anniversary Corvette." Dec. 1977, pp. 60-61.

"Corvette's 25th." C. Paul Rogers. Dec. 1977, pp. 62-66.

"'78 Chevrolet." Bob Hall. Oct. 1977, pp. 43-44.

"Plastic Futures." Aug. 1978, p. 27.

"The Turbine Corvette." Peter Frey. Nov. 1979, pp. 51-57.

"Fantasy Flagships." Leon Mandel, Burge Hulett, and Peter Frey. Dec. 1979, pp. 20-32.

"The 1983 Corvette." Ro McGonegal. Aug. 1980, p. 13.

"1982 Corvette." Bob Nagy. Oct. 1981, pp. 47-49.

"Is this the '83 Corvette?" Jim McCraw. Jan. 1982, p. 17.

Road & Track Special Series: Corvette

"1957 Corvette F.I." John F. Katz. 1987 issue, pp. 56-63.

"The SR-2." John Lamm. 1987 issue, pp. 91-93.

"The Shark." John Lamm. 1987 issue, pp. 102-06.

"The Aerovette." John Lamm. 1987 issue, pp. 108-12.

Road & Track

"Chevrolet Corvette." Aug. 1953, pp. 38-39.

"The Chevrolet Corvette." John R. Bond. June 1954, pp. 7-9, 44.

"Road Testing the Corvette." June 1954, pp. 10-12.

"Road Testing the Nash Healey." June 1954, pp. 38-39.

"1968 Corvette." Ron Wakefield. Oct. 1967, pp. 26-30.

"Styling Analysis." Jonathan Thompson. Oct. 1967, pp. 28-29.

"350-HP Corvette." Jan. 1968, pp. 36-39.

"435-HP Corvette." Mar. 1969, pp. 30-32.

"Four Luxury GTs." June 1969, pp. 52-58.

"454 Corvette." Sep. 1970, pp. 73-75.

"More on Corvette." Sep. 1972, p. 132.

"American Works in Progress." John Lamm. Oct. 1977, pp. 139-42.

"Chevrolet Corvette." Apr. 1978, pp. 62-64.

"General Motors, 1979." John Lamm. Nov. 1978, pp. 74-76.

"Chevrolet Corvette." Nov. 1982, pp. 170-76.

"New Chevrolet Corvette." Mar. 1983, pp. 34-39.

"Corvette vs. Ferrari 308 GTBi Quattrovalvole vs. Porsche 928S vs. Porsche 944." Aug. 1983, pp. 52-59.

"Corvette vs. 300-ZX Turbo." Jan. 1984, pp. 38-45.

"Indy Corvette." Paul Lienert. Jan. 1986, p. 96.

"Corvette Comparison: 1986 Z51 vs. 1968 L88." Feb. 1986, pp. 38-46.

"Corvette Convertible." Steve Kimball. Feb. 1986, pp. 52-53.

"Corvette Indy." John Lamm. June 1986, pp. 50-51.

"Callaway Twin-Turbo Corvette." Oct. 1986, pp. 56-58.

"Mid-engine Vette going soft?" Paul Lienert. Jan. 1987, p. 126.
"Corvette Survey." May 1987, pp. 48-49.
"Back to the Mother Lode." Peter Egan. Aug. 1989, pp. 38-49.
"Callaway Twin-Turbo Corvette." May 1990, pp. 112-115.
"Acura NSX." Aug. 1990, pp. 46-55.
"Different Drummers." Douglas Kott. May 1991, pp. 58-65.
"Callaway CR-1." Joe Rusz. Feb. 1993, pp. 56-60.

Sports Cars Illustrated

"Chevrolet Corvette." Karl Ludvigsen. May 1956, pp. 24-27, 55.
"Corvette." Stephen F. Wilder. Dec. 1958, pp. 32-33.
"1960 Corvette." Karl Ludvigsen. Nov. 1959, pp. 31-32.
"Road Test: '59 Corvette." Stephen F. Wilder. Mar. 1959, pp. 18-20.
"Is This the Corvette in Your Future?" Dean Parker. Mar. 1959,
  pp. 21-23.
"Road Research Report: Chevrolet Corvette." Dec. 1960, pp. 42-47,
  102-104.

PHOTOGRAPHY CREDITS

© Christopher Bain: pp. 8, 9, 12, 13, 24, 25, 30 (both), 33, 34 (both), 44, 45, 51, 53 (all), 63 (all), 73 (both), 108, 117, 123, 125, 126

Chevrolet Motor Division, General Motors Corporation: pp. 1 (both), 3, 4, 5, 20, 21, 38, 39, 49 (top right), 72, 81, 89, 93 (both), 113, 140

© Steve Coonan: pp. 94, 98 (bottom right)

© Bill Erdman: pp. 6, 22, 23 (both), 28, 36, 47, 57, 64, 67, 75 (bottom left), 76, 92 (top right), 105 (bottom left), 127 (both), 128, 129

© Steve Greenwood: p. 37

© George Kamper: pp. 15, 31, 43, 73, 88, 104, 105 (top left), 120

Courtesy National Automotive History Collection, Detroit Public Library: pp. 27, 49 (bottom left), 68, 132, 137

© D. Randy Riggs: pp. 2, 10, 11, 17, 18, 21 (top left), 35, 40 (both), 41, 42 (both), 52, 54 (top right), 58, 59 (both), 60, 61, 62, 63 (top photos), 67, 69 (both), 71, 78, 79, 91, 100, 102, 103, 107 (both), 109, 111, 112 (both), 113, 114 (both), 115, 116 (both), 117, 119, 122, 130 (bottom right), 131, 141

Courtesy D. Randy Riggs/Chevrolet Motor Division, General Motors Corporation: pp. 75 (top left), 95, 97, 98 (top right), 130 (top right)

Chevrolet, Chevy, the Chevrolet bow tie emblem, Corvette, 'Vette, the Corvette emblem, Stingray, and the Corvette body designs are trademarks of Chevrolet Motor Division, General Motors Corporation, and used under license to the Michael Friedman Publishing Group, Inc.

INDEX